William Caryl Cornwell

Sound Money Monographs

William Caryl Cornwell

Sound Money Monographs

ISBN/EAN: 9783744730525

Printed in Europe, USA, Canada, Australia, Japan

Cover: Foto ©Suzi / pixelio.de

More available books at **www.hansebooks.com**

SOUND MONEY
MONOGRAPHS

BY

WILLIAM C. CORNWELL

President of The City Bank, Buffalo
Author of " The Currency and the Banking Law of
Canada," etc.

G. P. PUTNAM'S SONS

NEW YORK   LONDON
27 West Twenty-third Street   24 Bedford Street, Strand

The Knickerbocker Press

1897

The Knickerbocker Press, New York

The Addresses, Magazine Articles, and other Monographs in these pages date from 1892 to 1897. While they have no special serial connection, they embrace the leading points in the discussion of Currency Reform, and it is hoped may be of service in popular education.

CONTENTS.

THIRTY YEARS OF WAR CURRENCY *

FOLLOWING a great victory for national integrity and honesty, it is natural for our people to expect an industrial revival.

That this does not come promptly is because we are not favored freely with that essential factor, European investments in our securities, and the reason for this hesitation of foreign capital is that the Silver question has not been finally settled, and a permanent Gold Standard made secure beyond doubt. The underlying reason for continued uncertainty is our unsound currency, and until this is remedied we cannot hope for solid prosperity.

In the United States we are to-day trying to do what has failed of accomplishment in five centuries of world history.

We are staggering under an endeavor to make the state give the life of currency to a

* Address at the banquet of the Boston Merchants' Asssociation, January 15, 1897.

I

valueless corpse, when history has proved that the only function of Government, with reference to money, is to stamp upon the chosen metals design and denomination, as the certificate of weight and fineness.

The channels of trade are filled with a currency which, in principle, is unscientific and unsound—currency of a kind which was first emitted in the dark days of the republic under the pressure of an advancing enemy and an empty Treasury, but which was condemned even then, with tremendous energy, by the sound and patriotic statesmen of that great day. The echo of their utterances in the debate in Congress on the first Greenback issue resounds in our ears even now as the prophetic cry of Truth striving to keep her children from error.

BIRTH OF THE GREENBACK.

"The notes to be emitted will be lepers in the commercial world from the hour they are brought into it," was Roscoe Conkling's prophetic condemnation.

"It must inflict a stain upon national honor," said Fessenden of Maine.

"It is hard, very hard, that such a country, so powerful, so rich, so beloved, should be compelled to adopt a policy of even a questionable propriety. Is it necessary to suffer this stain upon our national honor?" said Charles Sumner of Massachusetts.

"I am opposed to the legal-tender clause. In my judgment it is dishonest," said Sheffield of Rhode Island. ——

And Morrill and Pendleton and Thomas and a host of others opposed the bill with strong argument and sound reasoning.

I have no words against the patriotism of the men who urged this measure. They had at heart the best interests of their country. Its most prominent defenders were among the first to advocate the retirement of the Greenbacks after the war, and they lamented the excess of issue and the refusal of the country to cancel, but the wild animals had been let loose, and there seems to have been no power to recapture them.

Before this, through the struggles of nearly a century, paper fiat money had been strictly avoided. Poor and weak as the nation was in 1812, it had gone through that war without resort to it. And in 1862, rich and strong, the great mistake was made of reliance upon legal tender. In spite of strenuous opposition, the bill passed. It authorized the issue of 150 millions of Greenbacks. It passed with solemn assurance on the part of those who advocated it that it was only temporary—a first offense, and that we dare not repeat it.

How weak is human nature! The fatal cup had been, reluctantly, held to the lips, and tasted with aversion. Not three months later another issue of 150 millions was made, with little opposition, and not long after still another.

FALLACY DEMONSTRATED.

The fallacy of this whole operation is seen when we consider that after these comparatively few millions had been thus raised, resort was had to taxation and bonds, which should have been done at first, and ten times the amount was thus legitimately obtained before the war was over.

As a result of the legal-tender forced loan, the currency of the nation sank in value, slowly but surely, and for 17 years was the football of speculation. For 11 years there was a mad carousal of inflation and high prices and, in 1873, a disastrous settling day. Millions and millions were wiped out and six long years of hard times ensued.

During this period earnest attempts were made to retire and cancel the legal tenders. Retirement was twice begun and as quickly stopped by the cry of the rag-money contingent. And when, in 1879, we safely accomplished resumption, this Illegitimate Expedient of War, the Greenback, became the corner-stone of our monetary structure, and to-day the parity with gold of all other of the millions and millions of American values depends upon the parity of the Greenback.

TRUE CHARACTER HIDDEN AFTER RESUMPTION.

The 346 million Greenbacks in circulation were forbidden to be cancelled, and ordered to be paid out whenever taken in. Backed as they were by the 100 million reserve and many more millions in the Treasury and by the expanding credit and growing wealth of the nation, their true character was hidden and they became beloved of the people. Like many other popular idols, however, they were unworthy of the confidence placed in them. They are just as false in principle to-day as when, at their birth, they received the hesitant acceptance or open denunciation of the statesmen of war times. False friends in prosperity, they have proven bitter enemies when revenue was declining and confidence was ebbing. Their fierce attacks upon the gold reserve have three times in three years brought us to the brink of insolvency, and they lurk to-day, behind more favorable conditions, ready at any time to renew the fearful operations of the endless chain.

FIAT POISON WORKING.

Like all evils tolerated, they have refused to remain stationary, but have steadily spread and the fiat disease has developed. The Greenback craze in 1874 swept over the country like a prairie fire and came near enveloping the Government. Scarcely was this suppressed when the free-coinage advocate loomed up out of the smoke of inflation—a veritable genie of evil. He was compromised with and the Bland-Allison bill was the result. The Government went into the silver purchasing business and began paying out good gold for pig silver and issuing metal fiat dollars, instead of paper ones. It was the old Greenback idea—one of the same brood of reptiles—only the scales on this one were of silver instead of green paper. This was kept up for 12 years, and we became the dumping-ground for a metal which under our vast and useless accumulation of it was steadily sinking in value thoughout the world. Then in 1890 the old fiat-money genie came to the front again. It was the Silver-Mine Owner dressed up and disguised as Popular Demand. He demanded justice for silver—amends for the crime of 1873—free coinage at 16 to 1. Once more our politicians, awe-stricken, capitulated, and agreed to purchase the entire product of the silver mines of the United States. We went back to the green paper—the Treasury note, twin brother of the Greenback, and full of fiat poison.

DANGER AHEAD—DISASTER.

Our fiat currency was now creeping up towards the 1000 million mark. We were pledged by every consideration of national honor to redeem every dollar in gold. We were afflicted by a powerful minority in our legislatures in favor of silver and repudiation. The reserve itself was growing inadequate and gold began to leave our shores under the natural effects of inflation.

Then the fangs of the old Greenback serpent again became visible. They had been concealed for years.

There is under our remarkable system only one place in the United States where gold can surely be obtained.

That place is the United States Treasury.

The Greenback demand note, payable in gold, once paid, must be paid out again, and may come back over and over again, each time clutching the gold and depleting the Treasury.

Although we had been issuing fiat silver since 1878, the amount of demand gold notes from 1879 to 1890, was limited to the original 346 millions and there seemed no doubt of the ability of the United States to meet all these in gold.

In 1890, however, the Sherman law began to create an unlimited supply of demand gold notes of the endless-chain variety, at the rate of 50 millions a year. Investors viewed the spectacle with doubt and alarm, and began to realize upon their American securities and take away the gold. This culminated in the panic of 1893, and brought us to the edge of the precipice overlooking the silver basis, where we have remained ever since.

EVIL FORCES STILL ALIVE.

All the fatal machinery for depleting the gold reserve is still in splendid working order. Since the resumption of specie payments up to the present time, every dollar of the whole issue of Greenbacks has been paid once in gold, and one-third of the issue has been paid twice, and yet the whole amount is still in existence.

A great popular election has declared unmistakably for a gold basis, but nothing thus far has been done to assure such a basis. We are still at the edge of the precipice. All the evil forces still exist to push us off.

WAR CURRENCY STILL OUR DEPENDENCE.

Our dependence to-day, after more than 30 years, is still upon the old war currency ; upon a small issue of over-secured and rigid National Bank notes, the outcome of war needs, and an enormous Government issue, partly fiat silver intrinsically worth 50 cents on the dollar, and partly fiat paper which is constantly threatening the gold reserve and checking confidence. No thinking citizen can doubt, in view of the facts presented, that something should be done with our currency.

CURRENCY REFORM.

I believe that the plan of reform should be presented by an expert commission of the highest ability obtainable. I am confident that such a body of men would have little difficulty in agreeing promptly as to the main points, and in soon arranging details. There can be no harm, however, in considering at this time the principal features of reform.

There is, I believe, but little difference of opinion among earnest thinkers on the question as to what should be done first. Practically all are agreed that the Greenbacks and the Treasury notes should be retired.

DELUSIONS.

And yet we have in our midst the Eastern Greenback lover, who is as dangerous to the existence of our commercial fabric as the Western and Southern free-silver advocate. He ranges himself on the side of sound money, when he is for the unsoundest kind of money, the paper fiat of a Government. He ranks himself for gold and voted for McKinley, but he scoffs at the idea of abolishing the paper, the Government paper, that is a sleepless enemy of gold, the daily menace to the gold reserve, a shadow upon the possibility of maintaining gold payments; and by his obstinacy he imperils the value of every form of investment in the United States, because the shadow of doubt as to the Government's gold payments extends over every promise to pay in the country and keeps the foreign investor aloof. In other words, every dollar of obligation not specifically payable in gold would sink with the Greenback if the Treasury was unable to redeem every note in gold.

FAULT OF GOVERNMENT CURRENCY.

Many people ask the question, " Why cannot a great Government with unlimited resources for taxation best maintain the note issue, which affects the daily life of the people?"

The answer is that the Government is made up of representatives of the people, chosen not for business but for political reasons, and wise action in finances is rarely attainable.

Many of our law-makers know what should
be done, but the fact stands that a few ignorant
or vicious legislators are enabled to block the
whole body of Congress. Besides, with the
most unanimous intention, Congress and the
Treasury have no way of finding out the needs
of commerce, and currency has essentially to do
with business, with commerce. The regulation
of it must be thoroughly in accord with the
needs and requirements of trade.

The Government bank has no depositors and
cannot get its notes into circulation through
depositors as business needs them. It has no
automatic method of getting information as to
how much money is needed by trade, and could
not act upon it if it had. The Secretary of the
Treasury, ostensible manager of the bank, has
his hands tied. The Government currency once
out, stays out. It drifts away from the towns
of the West and South to the great cities of the
east, and stays there to breed speculation from
unnatural plenty, while the farmers and traders
of the prairies and cotton fields are suffering
from contraction.

ORIGIN OF FREE-SILVER CRY.

Out of this agony of contraction and starving
scarcity of money goes up the cry (and it is an
honest cry) for more money. It grows steadily

—it sweeps into a whirlwind—a wild appeal; the demagogue twists it to his foul purpose and it becomes a demand, now for silver, now for paper fiat, for unlimited issue. It incites wide discontent, links itself with anarchy, captures one of the great political parties, and, for a time, threatens the very existence of the nation.

Do you think you have quieted the cry for more money? It never will be quiet until these people with a legitimate want have that want supplied in a legitimate way.

What are we going to do about it?

Is there no way of meeting this demand?

SOUND WAY TO MEET IT.

There is only one sound way to meet it, and that is through the bank note based on the general assets of the bank, and not on specially deposited bond security, as is the case with National Bank notes.

The State Bank circulation which was slowly perfecting itself before the war, producing in several States admirable results, while in others it was bad, was cut off by a war tax which instituted National Bank notes. These notes, issued against special security, and not against general assets, are rigid in volume.

ELASTIC CURRENCY.

Notes issued against security pledged and held specially, as are our Government bonds, are defective in a country requiring sensitive elasticity in its currency. Such a system fails to respond to the laws of trade and under it the volume of currency, if there is a profit in it, will be too great, and if there is no profit, it will shrink without regard to the needs of the community.

Our National Bank notes lack the vitalizing element of a good bank note—that of daily redemption. Being secured by a special deposit, and over-secured at that, nobody ever takes the trouble to redeem them, and the fine character which the redemption test gives is lost.

Inflation rushed them up to 360 millions, when Congress set a limit. After that, lack of profit rushed them down to 120 millions, and contraction of the currency would have been the result if the fiat silver dollars had not taken their place.

We need in this country a currency especially sensitive in the quality of elasticity, besides being absolutely secure. On account of great field and forest production, we require at certain seasons of the year a rapid and substantial increase in our medium of exchange, the volume of which should, to avoid inflation, as rapidly shrink when the need is past.

There has never been a chance for a good currency to take root in this country since the beginning of the war, because the question has been the football of politics, and Commerce has not been allowed to choose its own methods and perfect them as she always does when left to do so, and as she was doing before the war.

The currency of a country should be based upon actual possessions, upon wealth, not upon public debt, such as Government or State bonds.

Commerce itself furnishes a perfect basis for itself under natural laws.

Large commercial banks are the longest-lived and the soundest institutions known to human history, many of them outliving the change of Governments and the fall of dynasties. In our own country we have a number of flourishing banks that are older than the Government itself. Sound commercial banks are the custodians of the products of the labor of the people, and these products represent mainly all there is of wealth in a nation.

COMMERCIAL ASSETS THE BEST SECURITY.

The experience of the last fifty years among nations of high civilization proves that commercial assets, the representatives of these products, are the highest form of security for note circulation.

Notes issued by properly capitalized and in-spected banks to the extent of a proportion (possibly in the future the whole) of their paid up capital and made a first lien upon these commercial assets, have behind them the only true scientific basis for circulation in a country like ours—the basis being the product of the energy, the muscle and brain, of our people. Trade consists in the exchange of these pro-ducts. Banks are the natural facilitators of such exchange. They hold, in short bills-re-ceivable, the paper representatives of the pro-ducts themselves. As by the increase of products trade increases, so scientifically and naturally there is provided in an increase of assets a larger basis for note circulation. The means, then, to move the crops, that operation which produces the great annual money-squeeze in this country, is furnished by the crops themselves. What better basis for bank notes can be created than these quick assets, the 60- and 90- day bills of millions of people. These are the things that are paid in panics when everything else is in default.

VOLUME AUTOMATICALLY REGULATED.

The volume of such bank notes is absolutely regulated by trade, and no more of them can stay out than trade needs. Let us examine this operation. The bank issuing its own notes depends upon its business depositors or borrowers to take such of its notes as they need in their business. They in turn pay them out and the notes go the rounds until deposited in some other bank. All bank notes received by other banks, under this system, are treated just as though they were checks.

That is, any bank getting the notes of another bank will promptly send them in, every day, and get the money for them, so as to be prepared to meet its own notes, which it is continually seeking to put out. But it will not dare to put its own notes out beyond its power, daily, to redeem them.

The increase in the number of bank notes is regulated, consequently, by the requirements of trade, and the desire of the banks to get their own notes out because of the profit there is in them—the interest there is on them when they are out.

The decrease is effected by the pressure brought to bear by other banks who, striving to force their own notes out, send the notes of other banks in, and the total amount kept out can thus never be more than trade actually requires. The regulation of volume is automatic. There can never be inflation. There can never be contraction. When the crops are to be moved, the money will come out to move them. When the operation is over with, the bank currency returns as silently as it came. The whole movement is like the rise and fall of the resistless tide.

As far as security is concerned, the statistics of the Comptroller's office show that if every National Bank in the United States since the inception of the system had issued against assets the currency, which it did issue against bonds, and a guaranty fund much smaller than the one proposed hereafter had been maintained, every dollar of notes of failed banks would have been redeemed in full throughout the whole period.

PERFECT THE NATIONAL SYSTEM.

Graft this principle upon the National system, which is great in every quality except that of circulation. Abolish or reduce the tax on circulation. Drop the United States bond special security—adopt the general security principle, making the note a first lien on all assets, including double liability of stockholders, limiting its issue to a percentage of capital, with a five per cent. guaranty fund maintained; all notes to be printed by the Government as now; all notes to be redeemable, daily, in gold, by the banks themselves, and through redemption agencies at the financial centres throughout the United States.

LARGE BANKS ONLY TO ISSUE.

The question of whether all banks, small as well as great, should issue currency, is one to be carefully considered. My own opinion is that only banks of large capital should issue notes. I am not in favor of following blindly the system of any other country, but am satisfied that the problem must be worked out slowly for ourselves, with reference to our own conditions. I believe, however, that if branches were permitted to the larger banks, the smallest towns and sparsely settled regions would get the fullest benefit. Allow banks say of not less than $1,000,000 capital to issue notes and have branches, but said branches to be located only in the State in which the head banks are respectively established ; banks, however, with $10,000,000 capital and with head offices in New York City to be allowed branches in all parts of the Union.*

EXPENSES SAVED AND PEOPLE BENEFITED.

By pledge of general security, the principle of elasticity thus scientifically carried out, under

---

* Suggestion of B. E. Walker, Esq., of the Canadian Bank of Commerce.

the fire test of daily redemption, would suppress inflation and foster enterprise in the South and West as well as in the North and East. Rates for money would be equalized and lessened, and new regions would be constantly developed. The immense saving of interest by this method would, eventually benefit the whole people.

THRIFT ENCOURAGED—NEW TERRITORY OPENED—FREE SILVER FALLACY SUPPRESSED.

Branches established in the small communities would, even without deposits at first, begin at once to develop the region covered. It would not be necessary to wait for deposits, as the bank notes could be loaned out at once on good security. Crops could be grown and cattle fed and goods conveyed to market by this means in communities where now they are barren of money and enterprise is stagnant. The people benefited would soon learn to deposit money, and thrift and wealth would follow. Without the note-issuing and branch system, such things are almost impossible. The dearth of money and credit in these far-off communities would be banished, populist fallacies would diminish, and the cry for free silver would die out.

SOUND CURRENCY AT LAST.

Instead of a war currency, devised not for the purposes of trade, but to appease the sharp

tooth of gaunt necessity, and clung to long
years after the least excuse for its existence
had vanished—a currency, clumsy, inadequate,
unscientific, and dishonest, partly founded upon
a war debt, but mostly the debt itself made
legal tender, or added to in kind and variety
as the years went by, all of it unsuited to our
needs,—instead of all this, we should have at
last a currency, secure, elastic, uniform, and convertible into gold on demand, and Commerce
in the United States would once more confi-
dently resume her sway.

GREENBACKS*

THE CAUSE OF ALL OUR TROUBLE AND THE
SOURCE OF THE SILVER CRAZE.

PART I.—THE GOLD RESERVE.

THE Gold Reserve is a sum of gold coin kept in the United States Treasury with which to pay Government bank notes, whenever anybody wants gold for them.

The intention of the Government is to keep this fund at not less than one hundred millions ($100,000,000).

The keeping up of this fund is what keeps us on a gold basis.

———

When the amount of United States notes was small, nobody paid any attention to the Reserve.

* *Greenbacks* was issued originally as an illustrated pamphlet, during the campaign of 1896. It was sold by the American News Company and reached its twenty-seventh thousand before election.

But when the amount got up to nearly a thousand millions, and was constantly increasing, people were afraid the Government could not keep enough gold to redeem the paper with.

Then everybody who knew anything about the situation began to watch the Gold Reserve.

This began in 1890, and has kept up ever since.

It was fear about the Gold Reserve that made the panic of 1893.

———————

The condition of all business in the United States to-day depends upon the Gold Reserve.

When the Reserve is full, and it looks as though it might be kept so, business revives and increases.

When the Reserve goes down, or is threatened, business stops, and we get along towards panic.

The Reserve got low in 1895, and we were saved from another panic by the President and the Bond Syndicate.

The Reserve dropped below a hundred millions a short time ago, and trouble was staved off by the banks and the foreign bankers, who chipped in and made the Reserve good.

How long will the business men of the United States stand this?

Upon the success of the business men depends also the success of clerks, mechanics, laborers, and farmers.

How long will all these let the wobbling Gold Reserve place the results of their hard work in danger?

HOW TO ABOLISH IT.

The remedy is a simple one.
The Gold Reserve is made necessary by the Greenbacks.

Pay up the Greenbacks, or even begin to cancel them, and prosperity is assured.

The Greenback has made possible the question of Free Coinage of Silver.

If there had been no Greenbacks, nobody would have questioned the advisability of the Gold Standard in the United States.

If the Greenback had been paid up after the resumption of specie payments in 1879, business would have grown better and better, the nation would have become richer every day, there would have been no Government Reserve to worry about, and the security of our currency would never have been doubted.

The panic of 1893 would have been avoided and the hard times since, during which silver has taken its strongest hold.

PART II.—HISTORY OF THE GREENBACK.

Greenbacks were first issued in 1862.

They were Fiat money.

The Government said to the people : " Here ; we want your produce, horses, mules, clothing ; we will give you for it paper, with the printed promise of a dollar on it, and will pass a law saying that it is good to pay all debts with. This will be a dollar."

The statement was a lie.

Some people believed the statement, and some did n't, but everybody *had* to take the dollar, and give up in exchange for it some kind of value.

The Greenback is Fiat money.

Making Fiat money is an attempt to make something out of nothing.

It is an attempt to create.

There is only one Creator.

Fiat money is a mild form of robbery.

It is a roundabout way of Governments confiscating the property of the people; is generally intended to be temporary, and is undertaken in great emergencies, like civil and other wars.

This is done for the benefit of the Government.*

Fiat-money confiscation is generally intended to be temporary, on the ground that if you have taken away a man's property because you thought it absolutely necessary, it is the proper thing when the necessity has passed to restore it to him.

England borrowed heavily from the Bank of England for the purpose of war with the French Republic in 1797, and went on to a paper basis in consequence.

France borrowed enormously of the Bank of France in the Franco-German war of 1870, and was forced to suspend specie payments.

* The free-silver people want this confiscation in time of peace—not for the benefit of the Government, but for the benefit of silver-bullion owners.

The confiscation in the case of paper Fiat currency, like the Greenback, is 100 cents on the dollar, as the paper is worth nothing.

The confiscation under free coinage would be 47 cents, as the silver bullion in the dollar would be worth 53 cents.

The silver-mine owners would get the 47 cents.

Russia, Austria, Italy, have all done the same.

All of these great nations, however, immediately after the close of the war, began the operation of retiring this legal-tender paper-money.

Four years after the close of war, England had retired all of hers.

Eight years after peace, France had paid up every dollar.

Thirty years have passed, and the United States floating war debt is not paid.

This is foolish and criminal negligence.

Worse than that, millions and millions of the same kind of money have been manufactured and issued since.

It is the fatal spread of the Fiat principle.

The Fiat principle is to a nation what the whiskey habit is to men.

It got possession of the United States when the first Greenback was rolled off the Government printing-press.

It is in possession to-day.

PART III.—CONTINUATION OF THE HISTORY
OF THE GREENBACK.

The Greenback cost the people during the war and until the time of resumption, hundreds of millions, as a result of inflation.*

The total issue of Greenbacks was 450 millions. In 1865, Congress ordered their gradual retirement. This was soon stopped, however, and more were issued.

In 1875, provision was made for specie payments, and again for the partial retirement of the Greenback.

But, the National Whiskey Habit developed once more in the " Greenback craze," and although this was crushed out, the fatal concession was made in 1878 **which prohibited further cancellation, and commanded re-issue of the Greenback, whenever and from wherever paid into the Treasury.**

* The total expenditure of the four years was $3,352,380,410, of which it is safe to say that $2,500,000,000 consisted of purchases in the open market, when the Greenback dollar procured only 66 cents' worth of property. In other words, we obligated ourselves for $2,500,000,000, and got $1,630,000,000 in actual value. The difference, $870,000,000, is the unnecessary cost to the taxpayers caused by the use of a depreciated currency—Horace White, *Money and Banking.*

"1878 SILVER." THE GREENBACK THE FATHER OF THE "SILVER SNAKE."

The Bland law of 1878 was a result of the Fiat principle established by the Greenback.

It was an outcome of the fatuous belief that the Government can and ought to create money, and was used by the silver-mine owners to make the United States buy their wares.

Under this law the United States agreed to buy 2 million dollars' worth of silver a month.

Why did the silver-mine owners not do something before 1878?

Why did they not oppose the Demonetization Act of 1873?

Because in 1873 the amount of silver in a dollar *was worth more than* 100 *cents gold in the market, and they did not wish to sell to the Government at a loss.*

But in 1876 the price of silver had gone down in the market, and the silver-mine owners began to agitate for free coinage.

If they could restore free coinage, they would make the Public buy all their silver above the market price and they would pocket the profit.

They were not able to restore free coinage.

The Bland Act of 1878 went half way. It made it necessary for the Government to purchase at least two million dollars' ($2,000,000) worth of silver a month at the market price.

The production then in the United States was about 3 millions per month.

The silver miners having made a Government market for two-thirds of their product, were satisfied for a time.

Disaster was predicted by the wise, as the outcome of this inflation of the currency of the country, but up to 1890 it had not come, because of big crops, and because National Bank notes not being profitable, had been retired by the banks to the extent of 200 millions, silver taking their place.

The currency was inflated under this act to the extent of 378 million Fiat silver dollars.

"1890 SILVER."

But by 1890 the production of silver from the mines had increased to over 4 millions a month.

By 1890 the Fiat principle had developed ·seriously.

The silver-mine owners had been doing all they could to develop it.

They now demanded free coinage.

They demanded it on what they pretended were high moral grounds, to make amends for the " crime of 1873," but really so that the mine owners might sell their whole product to the Treasury.

Congress was so afraid of the Fiat principle that a most disastrous compromise was effected. It was full of inflation and weak finance.

It obliged the Government to buy 54 million ounces of silver a year.

The total product of all the silver mines in the United States the year before was only 50 million ounces.

So this law unloaded onto the Treasury every dollar of silver that the mine owners could get out.

The Treasury was " held up " by the Silver Kings.

This was the " crime of 1890."

THE CRIME OF 1890.

Instead of coining silver into dollars under. this act, the bullion was to be bought " out and out " and paid for in Treasury notes, which were really Greenbacks.

This was the Law of 1890.

That was the time when the silver heresy should have been fought to a finish, and the Fiat-Silver principle crushed out.

It was an era of good times. The silver heresy had not taken root. The silver-mine owners were then the only ones really interested. Hard times have since helped them to many converts.

But the fight was not made.

Under the 1890 Law purchases of silver were doubled, and the bullion piled up.

In 1893 the pile fell over.

It crushed commerce. Stagnation, poverty, and misery followed and are still with us.

1893.

The people, convinced that Fiat money was the root of all the trouble, rose in their might and insisted that the deal with the silver miners should be closed, and the purchase of silver stopped.

The purchase was stopped.

But we had gone already too far.

The Fiat money in the United States, issued up to that time and still in existence, foots up as follows:

Greenbacks, 346 millions -
Treasury notes, act of 1890, 156 } Redeemable
millions   -   -   -   -   in gold.

Silver dollars under act of 1878, } Must be kept
378 millions   -   -   -   at par with gold.

In all nearly 900 millions depending upon the slender gold reserve, to say nothing of National Bank notes, which indirectly lean upon it too.

PART IV.—FIAT MONEY THE DISEASE—HOW IT AFFECTS BUSINESS.

Fiat money is the disease.

Let us see how we suffer from it to-day.

We need gold at certain seasons to pay debts to foreign nations.

In other countries they go to the banks for this gold.*

* In any country where the banks are looked to for gold for export, these institutions have within their own hands the means of controlling such export. If gold begins to go out unduly, they can raise the rate on money, and by this method of calling in loans, moderately and automatically, stop the purchase of imports. High rates for discount, and

There is only one sure place to go for gold in the United States.

That place is the United States Treasury.

The Greenback is a demand note payable in gold.

When the Government has paid it once in gold it must pay it out again.

The same note will again be presented and gold demanded. Gold must be paid once more, and so on forever.

This is the endless chain.

There are 346 million Greenbacks and 156 million Treasury notes about the same in character.

Five hundred millions in all payable in gold on demand and payable over and over again.

The Gold Reserve of 100 millions is depended upon to supply this voracious demand.

curtailment of loans, tend to make holders reduce prices of securities and commodities in order to effect sales and realize cash. The low prices thus brought about produce exports by inducing foreign purchase of produce, stocks, and bonds ; these go out instead of gold, and meanwhile foreign capital comes in, attracted by profitable investment at higher rates for money.

When the Reserve begins to sink, there is only one way to replenish it. That is by buying gold with Government bonds. 262 millions have been issued in two years for this purpose, and the other day the stock of gold was once more under the 100.

If the Government cannot redeem in gold every dollar of obligation presented for redemption, we drop to repudiation.

Upon this shifty expedient, the shifting Gold Reserve, we depend to maintain the credit of the nation.

The Reserve then is the big barometer of the commercial atmosphere. Everybody in this country and in Europe is forever anxiously watching it; the capitalist, the money lender, the bank manager, the business man—always looking in the newspaper to see how the Reserve stands; and all smile or look sorry as it shows high or low. If below the limit, the question from day to day is, "What shall be done?" Enterprise wilts; business stops short; Europe sells our securities; we are in the gloom of coming storm.

FUSI YAMA.

In Japan a magnificent volcano rises out of the Pacific Ocean.

Its top is covered with snow.

It is an object of worship and veneration.

People watch its slightest change, for it means to them good or bad fortune.

Its name is Fusi Yama.

It is the mountain idol of Japan.*

The Treasury Reserve of the United States is the Fusi Yama of business in America.

Night and morning we look to it with fear and trembling, like that of the heathen of Japan.

It is not surprising that the nations of the world, educated by past history and the experience of generations, look on in mild amazement at the spectacle of a great people, tolerating, nay clinging with childish affection to such a system ; they look on, but since 1890 the

---

*In far-off Japan, out of the waters of the Pacific, there rises a magnificent volcano, higher than any other mountain, and completely dwarfing all other eminences on the horizon. Snows of an arctic region rest upon its rounded crest, and bathed in eternal sunshine it glistens in the bright rays like molten gold.   It is the everlasting theme of poetry and art, and has for centuries been the object of worship and religious awe. Thousands of pilgrims annually make ascent to the line of snow, and the whole nation watches with veneration and reverence for the slightest change in its aspect as indicative of weal or woe.

This is Fusi Yama, the gold-crowned mountain idol of Japan.—*Greenbacks and Legislation*, AUTHOR.

capitalists of Europe have taken good care to avoid investing with us, and this they will continue to do until our temporary insanity is permanently cured.

INSUFFICIENT REVENUE.

Does lack of revenue play no part in this loss of confidence?

Yes, it certainly does. It plays the part *that added weight does in helping the fall of the building when the foundation is rotten.*

It is an incident, not the cause.*

* Let us look at the facts :

Up to 1890, although we had been purchasing silver since 1878, Fiat money had not been issued to such an alarming extent as to make it seem to the impartial, unprejudiced outside observer, that the United States Government would be unable to pay all its obligations in gold. In fact, up to 1890, the amount of demand notes payable in gold was limited to three hundred and forty-six millions—that is, to the issue of Green-backs which had not been cancelled in 1878, when the law to stop went into effect.

THE BREAK OF CONFIDENCE.

In 1890, however, Congress passed a law which made it necessary for the Government to issue over $50,000,000 a year in Treasury notes, payable in gold. Thinkers and investors throughout the world turned to the spectacle, and asked the question, whether the United States, strong and great as she was, could maintain an unlimited issue of demand notes, payable in gold, which might be presented again and again,

There never was in the mind of the foreigner any doubt as to the United States being able to raise enough revenue to pay expenses.

So simple a problem as our ability by legislation to tax for this purpose never disturbed him.

What the foreigner doubted was whether we (with no means of getting gold except on bonds) could maintain on a level with gold a vast mass of Fiat money, hundreds of millions of dollars already, more and more being produced every year for an indefinite period. That was the question that worried the foreign investor in 1890, '91, '92, that worries him now, that worries us all.

PART V.—ABOLISH THE GOLD RESERVE—AN APPEAL TO CONGRESS.

If the fetish of the Gold Reserve were taken away and Europe were but assured that the

and must again and again be paid out after being redeemed. When that question came to be pondered in Europe, our securities began to come home ; our cash and our gold began to go out ; the Reserve began to be trended upon, and that condition has continued ever since. In the latter part of 1893, the purchase of silver was stopped, but by that time so many notes had been issued, and in view of the law of 1890, declaring the Government's intention to keep all its currency at par with gold (including silver certificates), a problem was presented which failed to restore the confidence of investors abroad and of those at home.—*Greenbacks and Legislation.*

three, four, or five per cent, interest obtainable within our shores was positively, permanently, and forever a gold investment, the stream of yellow metal would flow to us from all the peoples of the world and cheer and unending prosperity would roll in upon the shining flood.

How can we rid ourselves of this panic-producing Reserve?

Clearly, only by abolishing that which makes the Reserve necessary, namely, the demand gold-notes of the Government.

A request was sent to Congress on this subject last winter. It embodied these suggestions for immediate financial legislation :

" First. Provide for the redemption and cancellation of the Greenback to the extent of one hundred millions within one year, and one hundred millions during each succeeding year until three hundred millions of the Greenbacks are retired ; then include in the cancellation also Treasury notes until the entire five hundred millions of Government paper have been extinguished.

" To provide funds for these operations, issue low-rate long-time gold bonds.

" Second. As to what shall take the place of the Government paper thus extinguished, appoint at once a non-partisan expert currency commission to decide."

It was accompanied by the following argument :

" We ask to have the Reserve abolished, because fear as to the Reserve has broken confidence at home and abroad, stagnating business, holding off prosperity.

" We ask to have the Government notes abolished, because their existence makes a Reserve necessary.

" We ask for their retirement gradually only, knowing that the *declared intention* of this great Government to wipe out *all* its gold-demand notes, would be a declaration unmistakable for the gold standard, and would instantly restore confidence in us throughout the world.

" This done, gold would come in without stint, and an immense revival in trade would follow. Under these conditions, and, pending the decisions of an expert currency commission, the place of the Greenback, if currency was needed, would be filled by the most desirable of all mediums—the gold itself."

PART VI.—THE APPEAL NOT HEEDED—THE DISEASE DEVELOPS—FREE SILVER.

The petition was unheeded.

Nothing was done to establish the certainty of the gold standard.

Eight months have passed.

Naturally capital at home and abroad has not gained confidence, and business enterprise has been shut off.

The times have consequently grown harder, and in hard times financial heresies flourish best.

To-day the Fiat Disease has developed into a fever.

THE PRESENT SITUATION.

It has pulled around itself the cloak of a great party, hiding its hideous features.

Once more the demand for Free Coinage at the old ratio of 16 to 1.

It is still the silver-mine owners, shut off in 1893 and hungry for the spoils.

But with them are the poverty-stricken, the discouraged, the debt-ridden, the rainbow-chasers, the false theorist, the place-hunters, the dyed-in-the-wool politician, speculators, repudiators, and many desiring to be honest but deluded by superficial promises of prosperity.

Deluded with the belief that law can change value.

That the United States can decree silver equal to gold, and make it so in the markets of the world.

The demand is for Free Coinage at 16 to 1.

16 TO 1.

That is that 16 oz. of silver shall equal 1 oz. of gold.

But in the markets of the world it takes 31 ounces of silver to equal 1 ounce of gold.

What is the process under free coinage?

Why, you buy $1000 worth of silver bullion. You take it to the mint and have it coined into nearly 2000 silver dollars.

Who can do this?

Any one who has the silver bullion.

Who has the silver bullion?

No one in any quantity—except the silver-mine owners.

It is the same old crowd who held up the Treasury in 1878 and in 1890.

They are creating once more a market for their wares.

But who has to stand the expense?

The people of the United States—the masses.

Then it IS "the classes against the masses"?

Yes, but the silver party represents the classes and the gold-standard people the masses.

SILVER FREE.

Some people think that free silver means that money will be free to every one.

This is, of course, nonsense. It will take the same hard work to get money then as now.

But the money, when gotten, will be worth only half as much.

Promises of abundant money under free silver are false.

No free-silver country ever had abundant money.

The present silver dollar, although really worth only 53 cents, is kept at par by the guaranty of the United States to keep it so, and the belief in the ability of the Government to do this.

Under free coinage, the Government could not possibly keep the silver at par with gold, as the amount would be unlimited; even now with a limited amount it is difficult to keep up the Reserve, as we have shown.

Consequently the value of all silver dollars would be cut in two.

The 1,100 millions in circulation would thus be cut down to 550 millions.

The 600 million gold now in circulation would instantly disappear, as it would be worth twice as much as silver and nobody would, under those circumstances, pay it out.

So that immediately upon the adoption of free coinage, the amount of money in use would be cut down from 1700 millions to 550 millions actual value.

This does not look like keeping promises, as to more money.

What we want is more capital, not more money, not cheap 50-cent dollars.

We want the capital that has been withdrawn since 1890 returned to us.

The capital will come from the whole world the moment it is assured as to our gold basis.

HIGHER PRICES.

Higher prices are promised by the silver people.

These will come.

It will take two of the cheap dollars to purchase as much as one good dollar does now.

But all wages, salaries, and incomes will be paid in the *cheap dollars.*

What does the workman (high or low in the labor ranks) say to this?

It is true.

A vote for free coinage means a vote to increase, to double, perhaps, the cost of all household expenses, the necessities of life, without the power to add one cent to wages, salaries, or income.

TO THE LABORING MAN.

With a given quantity of gold, more necessary things can be bought now than twenty years ago.

But a given quantity of labor will command a larger quantity of gold *now* than *then*.

What does the laboring man say to that?

He can now get more things for gold, and more gold for his labor than in 1873.

The gold standard dollar of to-day will buy less labor and more goods than any dollar in the history of the world.

Does the laborer want the free-coinage dollar, which is the gold dollar cut in two?

TO DEBTORS.

The silver people say they are working in the interest of the debtor.

That means that they will make it legal for the debtor to pay up in full at 50 cents on the dollar.

This is true.

But who will stand the difference?

Who will be "out" the other 50 cents?

Here is a partial table of those who will suffer:

Depositors in Loan Associations, Savings Banks, Banks, etc.,
10 million people of all classes, principally wage earners
and people with small incomes—
Amount of deposits...................... $5,350,000,000
Value, cut in two, under free coinage....... 2,675,000,000

Loss to the people noted above........ $2,675,000,000

Beneficiaries of Life-Insurance Policies, 13 million of people—
Amount of policies....................... $10,204,000,000
Value, cut in two, under free coinage....... 5,102,000,000

Loss to beneficiaries, widows and orphans,.. $ 5,102,000,000

This is only a partial list of the sufferers who
will help out the debtor.

It is repudiation pure and simple.

A SIREN.

The picture presented to us is of a charming
siren dispensing broadcast the pleasures of life.
Back of it all is a skeleton.
That skeleton is naked Repudiation of Debt.

PART VII.—PROSPERITY 1879 TO 1890.

The gold standard unwaveringly maintained has always brought prosperity in the United States.

It was the doubt about it that blighted prosperity in 1890, and the continuing

doubt since then that has steadily invited adversity.

Wheat was maintained at an average of 71½ cents (gold) per bushel on the farm from 1862 to 1890.

The farmer had nothing to complain of until after 1890.

It is since then that the serious decline in the United States has come.

As for the workman (and this includes all classes of labor), there never was a time in the history of the world when he could earn so many comforts and luxuries with his salary, earnings, or wages as he could in 1890, and a little later, until the effect of *doubt about the gold standard* began to be felt.

THE GOLD STANDARD NECESSARY TO PROSPERITY.

If the absolute stability of the gold standard in this country is assured, prosperity will once more return, and in no other way can it be secured.

Here is what M. Leroy Beaulieu, the distinguished French economist, a man absolutely unprejudiced, says, in *The Forum :*

" If the United States are to maintain a commercial, and still more a financial position equal to that of England, the dollar must be given the qualities of the pound sterling ; that is, there must be no sort of doubt that it is a gold dollar, and that never for any reason or under any pretext that which is called a dollar shall be paid in silver. Then all nations will have the same faith in the dollar that they have in the pound sterling. As the United States have a territory infinitely more vast than that of England, a territory full of the most varied resources, and in which capital can find great opportunities of profit, that country will become the chosen land for the capital of the whole world. . . . All that is lacking is a completely solid monetary system to enable the American people to profit by a large part of the capital accumulated in such enormous quantities by the old nations of Europe. . . .

" So soon as the capitalists, small and great, of Europe, shall know that the United States have definitely adopted the gold standard and relegated silver to a subordinate monetary role, the savings of Western Europe will flow toward that country. Freed from the fear that he may some day be repaid in depreciated money, every person with savings in all Europe will be happy to find a return of 3½ to 4 per cent. in good American securities, and 5 to 5½ per cent. in the shares of well established American enterprises. Then the immense territory of the United States will find its vast resources rapidly and completely put in the way of exploitation.

" **The abandonment of notes or paper money issued by the State (Government) ; the definitive adoption of gold as the sole standard,**—these are the two necessary conditions on which the United States can secure a financial position as important as that they now hold in agriculture and in industry."

In the face of these sober, deliberate, and unprejudiced statements of the truth, we are asked to start out in pursuit of a will-of-the-wisp.

A WILD CHASE.

The Chicago platform perched upon the shoulders of unwilling Democracy, backed by the death's head of Populism and Anarchy, is riding rough-shod over stricken Commerce, out into the abyss spanned part way by a single plank, in wild pursuit of the lovely and seduct- ive form of Fortune, who floats serenely onward perched upon the bubble of Fiat money and holding out the false light of Free Silver.

It is in this wild chase that the sober, think- ing people of America are asked to join.

THE QUESTION WILL BE UNDERSTOOD.

The money question is a deep and puzzling one.

But our thinking, sober, honest people are bound to understand it.

They cannot be long deluded with false reasoning.

Our greatest leader, he who perhaps of all our public men, understood the American peo- ple best, said of them : " You can fool some of them all the time ; and all of them some of the time ; but you cannot fool all of them all the time."

PART VIII.—CONCLUSIONS—1879 TO 1890, PROSPERITY—1890 TO DATE, ADVERSITY.

Since 1873 the United States has been on a gold basis by law, and since 1879, when specie payments were resumed, on a gold basis in fact.

From 1879 to 1890, at home and abroad, confidence in our intention and ability to adhere to the gold standard was absolute.

During that period the United States was more prosperous than at any other time in its history, all classes of workers were comfortable, happy, and better paid than ever before, and the national wealth increased to an enormous extent.

SINCE 1890.

Since 1890 the gold standard has been in question; due to non-payment of the floating war debt—the Greenbacks—which allowed the Fiat-money idea to obtain root and expand under pressure from the silver-mine owners, into Fiat-Silver Legislation. This loaded up our currency system with inflated issues, and culminated in the Purchase Act of 1890, which absorbed the entire product of the silver mines, continuing the inflation of the currency to an enormous extent.

In 1890, confidence in our ability to maintain our currency on a gold basis broke, foreign

4

capital began to be withdrawn, panic ensued, hard times settled down, and hard times will stay until conditions are reversed.

Two things are needed for assured prosperity.

An overwhelming victory for the Gold Standard this fall.

This will at once start the flow of foreign capital this way.

Second.   Legislation for the retirement of gold-demand fiat-money, the Greenbacks and the Treasury notes.

This will keep it coming.

THE GOLD BASIS IN THE UNITED STATES IS THE CAUSE OF OUR MARVELLOUS PROS-PERITY FROM 1879 TO 1890.

THE ATTEMPT TO ESTABLISH A SILVER BASIS, THROWING DOUBT ON THE GOLD BASIS, IS THE CAUSE OF HARD TIMES FROM 1890 UP TO DATE.

THE GREATER THE DEFEAT OF THE CHICAGO PLATFORM IN NO-VEMBER, THE LARGER WILL BE THE SHARE OF PROSPERITY TO EVERY CITIZEN IN THE UNITED STATES.

CURRENCY REFORM *

THE currency question, one of the most important to the welfare of any nation, has never been satisfactorily settled in the United States.

For more than a hundred years its history is a record of experiments and temporary expedients without a single adequate solution.

No country is so full of currency doctors as ours, and we have finally evolved nine different kinds of money, nearly all diseased. In the meantime the commerce of the country has gone on increasing enormously, with the effect that at regular or irregular periods we have some such a tremendous fit of sickness as that through which we are just passing.

The cause is physical—there is poison in the blood. Everything is all right except the circulation ; that is diseased.

It is to be hoped that the people are now so thoroughly aroused to the facts that they will

* Address at the Convention of the American Bankers' Association, Chicago, October 18, 1893. (Previous to the repeal of the purchasing clause of the Sherman act).

insist upon a complete revision of the currency system, going to the very bottom of things, and placing the commerce of the country on the most perfect monetary foundation which the expert financial wisdom of this century can construct.

I cannot hope to say anything new on this subject, but a presentation of the salient points, the essential requirements, the indisputable errors, as they are generally agreed to by nearly all thoughtful students of our conditions, cannot fail to do good.

It is perhaps well enough to recall at this point one or two essential principles as to currency that all history has proven true.

It is the province of a government to stamp value upon precious metals, thus creating coin out of the bullion belonging to the people and for their uses, but beyond this no government can properly or honestly go. The arbitrary creation of paper currency by a government is an abuse of power, which is always punished in proportion to the amount issued. Such a manufacture of so-called money is against all principles of science and experience.

Commerce is the exchange of products created by the exercise of human brain and muscle. Currency is merely the representative of these products, facilitating the exchange of

them. The moment currency ceases to represent products it becomes bad currency. Indi-
viduals can produce—governments cannot—
they can only tax. Hence government currency, like our Greenbacks, an arbitrary creation
issued against nothing but credit, is false in
principle and a hollow dependence.

Currency being solely a facilitator of commerce, should be regulated solely by the needs
of commerce, but in this country politics has
been the main consideration, and a deplorable
condition of things is the result.

I have spoken of our currency system as in
a diseased state. The existing causes may be
listed as follows:

CAUSES.

First, Silver Legislation.

Second, Greenbacks and Treasury Notes.

Third, National Bank Notes because over-
secure.

Fourth, Suppression of Bank Currency.

SILVER LEGISLATION.

Little need be said as to silver. The country
has received such an education in the last six
months as it will not soon forget.

One thing should be emphasized at this
point in the struggle: *Silver-Bullion buying is
the cause of the recent panic.* The fact that

this country was apparently in the full whirl of prosperity last October is no argument. The steam engine just before explosion is running at greatest pressure—it is then that false metal in the boiler yields. Bullion buying, more than three years ago, caused foreign buying of our securities to cease and foreign selling to begin, along with gold exports, and decrease in treasury gold reserve. Financiers during this whole period have been calling attention to this and predicting just such a state of things as has come about.

This is the turning point in the Nation's career from bad to good finance. At this juncture all eyes turn to one man. Unawed by threats of enemies, unmoved by the entreaties of political friends, unbiased by fears of party dissolution, with mind made up as to what was right, he has stood in the breach, almost alone at times. Had it not been for his indomitable will, we would be as far away as ever from a firm foundation. When the happenings of these times have crystallized into history, the name of Grover Cleveland will shine out clear, as the hero of the hour, the man whose courage stemmed the tide of shifting compromise, brought to naught the craft of trimming politicians, and saved the cause of honest money.

Bullion buying is the worst financial measure on the lowest possible motives ever undertaken in this country. Its stoppage is positively necessary for the arrest of disease. All other reforms must wait for this one. It is the poison in the circulation which, if not completely eradicated, will corrupt every remedy applied. Beyond all this, it is absolutely fatal to bimetallism, so-called, and those who deem themselves friends of silver as a money metal should remember this.

GREENBACKS AND TREASURY NOTES.

Under the second head of diseases of the country come the fiat issues of the Government, the Greenback and the Treasury Note.

The Greenback is the senior violator of the principle that a government should issue no paper money. 346,000,000 of them, the heritage of the war, are still with us. Since our resumption of specie payments they have stood up stiffly, and until recently have been accepted round the world as good as gold; but that does not one whit abate the fact that their issue is wrong in principle and a rotten element in our monetary make-up.

These are times when all fallacies heretofore tolerated, because they were not so very bad should be stricken out. We have had enough of criminal compromise. We have tried it with silver at a terrible cost. A thing is either right or wrong, and if wrong, wipe it out no matter how limited.

The Greenback is half-brother to rag money, born when the flag was in danger. It has managed thus far to appear in respectable garments, but its fiat character is visible to those who lift the coat flaps. The 100,000,000 gold reserve and the credit of the Government have kept it in countenance until recently, when the other fiat money, the paper silver, fell back with a dull thud on that same hundred millions and there was an earthquake which shook the faith of many.

The Greenback must go if we desire to act upon an absolutely sound basis.

The Treasury notes, of which something over $140,000,000 have been issued under the Sherman Law, being legal tender and redeemable in gold (if there is any), add to the danger of fiat Government issues, begun by the 346,000,-000 greenbacks. We have here, both together, 486,000,000 of paper money issued by a government with less than 100,000,000 in gold to keep it perpendicular. Whether or not the government has the credit to do this, there comes a time (no man can predict the moment), as there came in June, when suddenly the people begin to doubt, there is one grand explosion, and when the smoke has cleared away the Demon of Distrust looms up, hovering over the ruins and carrying devastation as he sweeps his uncanny wings across a nation's commerce from ocean to ocean.

If the Greenback and the Treasury note are retired, as they should be, 500,000,000 of the currency is wiped out. Something must take its place.

NATIONAL BANK NOTES.

Let us take up now the National Bank note. Strange as it may seem, this popular bread buyer is the innocent cause of much of our trouble, on account of its unscientific character.

The apparent necessities of war gave birth to the national system as a proposed means of placing more Government bonds. The issues of all but National Banks were cut off by the ten per cent. tax, and National Banks were alone allowed to issue notes upon security of U. S. bonds at par for ninety per cent. of notes. The country was off a specie basis, so that there was no pressure to redeem, and the high rates of interest on the bonds made issue very profitable. The tendency then was towards inflation, and the total issue went up to 360,000,000, and had to be limited by Congress.

When Government rates decreased materially, the issue began to contract because there was no profit in it until in ten years it shrank to 120,000,000. When this decrease began a contraction of the currency followed, and that was the time when proper reform should have been introduced as to security, so that the full volume of bank currency could have been maintained and increased. Nothing of the kind was done, and the politican and the silver-miner jumped in to fill the gap caused by the contraction of 240,000,000 in bank currency. They filled it—and to-day we have about 500,000,000 of debased silver issues as a result.

The National Bank note is an over-secured fallacy, popular because of its abnormal development in one direction, that of security. It has back of it from 20% to 30% more than its face value in gold bonds. There is such a thing as being too good.

The National Bank note is too good.

The cost of developing it in that direction is so great that it lags, in a comatose state, under its great burden like a sturdy yeoman who has overdosed with morphine, or like the man in the cave of treasure who loaded up with so much precious metal that he could not move.

Additionally stupefying is the one per cent. tax on circulation.

The elastic quality is thus effectually obliterated.

A bank note should come out when needed by commerce, and retire after the need has passed. The National Bank note does neither one thing nor the other.

It lacks the vitalizing element of a good bank note—that of redemption. Being secured by a special deposit, and over-secured at that, nobody ever takes the trouble to redeem it, and the fine character which the redemption test gives is lost.

SUPPRESSION OF BANK ISSUES.

We come now to the fourth head. The ten per cent. tax confines bank issues to national notes, and these have been shown to be ineffectual. The thinking public has come to recognize the injustice of this suppression, and hence the clamor in many quarters for the repeal of the ten per cent. tax. Let us see what would be accomplished by bringing on State circulation.

Banking before the war was largely experimental. Each State tried one thing or another with variable degrees of success. A few States struck the right principle, and in two or three for a period of forty years the most exemplary success was achieved and maintained.

In other States there was no marked success, and in the majority the most decided lack of it. There never was any uniformity of system between States, and as to safety, in twenty or more this element was lacking.

If it is expected by reviving these varying systems to make such a national currency as we need, the expectation will only be fulfilled after a long period of evolution.

As to the rights of State banks, it is a very simple thing for a State bank to change to a National one, carrying its rights with it and no injustice done.

Admitting that the most perfect form of currency is the note of a good bank, how can you get your banks good before you allow them to issue?

Not certainly by throwing the control of them into the hands of forty-four different legislatures of all degrees of intelligence and political complexion, as would be done if the State tax were repealed.

For thirty years the National system has been perfecting its restrictions until to-day it shows a high standard of average strength and safety, and a record for the whole period of its existence which probably—taking number of banks and all, into consideration—is unequalled in the history of banking. This record is condensed in the statement of a recent comptroller that the total average of loss in the whole system for the whole time up to last year was only three per cent.

Here, then, is a system which, on one side, has been developed and perfected with the utmost care for thirty years by a succession of competent comptrollers, until on that side—the Department of Safety—it has attained a very high level. On the other side—that most important one—of circulation—there has been actually no development whatever.

REMEDIES.

The situation then condensed is as follows:

We desire to place our currency upon a sound basis, and while eliminating all false elements to maintain sufficient volume, with a provision for increase and a provision for elasticity.

In order to accomplish this: First of all, silver purchasing must cease; without this it is absolutely useless to institute other reforms.

Then our legal tenders, the Greenback and the Treasury Note must be retired.

This brings us to the question, What shall fill the gap thus created.

There is but one answer. The present tendency in all the great nations of the world is towards bank currency. Bank currency is what we, too, must depend upon. This is strictly in accordance with scientific sequences.

The wealth of a country should be the basis of its currency. The basis is furnished by commerce itself.

The products of the labor of the people represent all there is of financial value (wealth) in a nation. Commercial banks, the friends of all classes of the people, of the wage earner, the merchant, and the capitalist—commercial banks, the longest lived and soundest institutions known in history, are the custodians of the representatives of this wealth in the shape of commercial assets, and commercial assets, all time proves, are the highest form of security for note circulation.

Notes issued by properly capitalized and inspected banks to the extent of a proportion of their paid-up capital, and made a first lien upon their assets, not specially pledged, but held as general security, have behind them the only truly scientific basis for circulation in a country like ours—the basis being the product of the energy, the muscle, and brain of our people. Trade consists in the exchange of these products. Banks are the natural facilitators of such exchange. They hold, in short, bills-receivable, the paper representatives of the products themselves. As by the increase of products trade increases, so scientifically and naturally, there is produced in an increase of assets a larger basis for note circulation. The means to move the crops are furnished by the crops themselves. What better basis for bank notes can be created than these quick assets? Such bank notes, under regulations for daily redemption, modestly and automatically retire when they are not needed.

Graft this principle upon the National system. Abolish the over security and the tax on circulation. Make the note secure enough, but not too secure. Drop the United States bond special security—adopt the general security principle which is in such successful operation in Canada, making the note a first lien on all assets, including double liability of stock-holders, limiting its issue to a percentage of capital with a guarantee fund and other minor details to be arranged.

Establish redemption agencies at financial centers throughout the United States.

Let all notes be printed by the Government as now.

Under the general security principle, daily actual redemption would then become a fact. The operation would be the same as under the Canadian law.

In Canada, bank notes are redeemed every
day as checks. If a bank receives the notes
of other banks, it immediately sends them on
for redemption, paying out its own notes over
its counter in a daily endeavor to put them in
circulation. It is of course a direct benefit to
each bank to have as many of its own notes
out as it possibly can. Then with every bank
crowding for redemption and retirement all
the notes of every other bank, and pressing out
all it possibly can of its own, it is readily seen
that only the actual amount needed by commerce will stay out—that the amount will rise
and fall automatically with the actual business
demand or lack of it. This is the principle of
elasticity scientifically carried out, suppressing
inflation, fostering enterprise and working out
its own fine end under the fire-test of daily
redemption.

Would this currency meet in volume the requirements of the country?

There is no doubt about it. The redemption of the Greenback and the Treasury note,
$500,000,000 in all, could be accomplished
gradually, by the use of the $100,000,000 gold
reserve, by the sale of silver bullion, by means
of the debt sinking fund appropriation, by income, by borrowing on gold bonds for the purpose. This should be done gradually.

Meantime the National bank-note issues, relieved of heavy burdens, but protected and made absolutely safe, would increase, and as they did so the legal tender retirement could be kept automatically level with such increase. The volume of notes would also swell from rapid change of State banks into National and from new organizations. A few years would see the change completed.

We would then have for our main circulating medium a bank currency, absolutely secure, subject to daily redemption in specie, of uniform value in every part of the United States, and because of daily redemption possessing the necessary elasticity for the requirements of our commerce, at one time growing rapidly to meet its swelling volume, and afterwards sinking out of sight as the need subsided.

Trade could then go on, for the first time in the history of this country, unhindered by the fear of disturbance and corruption at its very base, sure of the essential foundation of all enduring commercial prosperity—a sound currency.

We could then take the lead as the foremost commercial nation of the earth, and it would not be long before the Dollar of the United States, instead of the Pound Sterling, would rule the world.

SYNOPSIS.

Present unsatisfactory conditions of the currency question in the United States.

Causes :
Silver legislation.
Legal tenders.
National bank-note regulations.
Suppression of bank currency.

Under first head all responsibility for present panic placed upon the Silver Purchase clause, claiming that no other reform will be of any avail until the poison of bullion buying is obliterated. The country warned that unqualified repeal of the Silver Purchase law must be carried out. Any compromise will be a compromise with poison.

LEGAL TENDERS.—The Greenbacks and the Treasury notes false in principle and a constant menace to the stability of the currency. They should be gradually retired.

NATIONAL BANK NOTES.—Their unscientific character. Their retirement because unprofitable opened the way for the Silver craze. Over-security, their great fault, excluding any possible elasticity.

BANK-NOTE SUPPRESSION.—The ten per cent. tax. Effect of its abolition. Unnecessary if the right principle of security is introduced into the National system, making bank issues profitable. State banks could then become National banks without trouble.

REMEDIES.

Stop buying silver.

Retire the Greenbacks and Treasury notes gradually, letting National notes under new regulations take their places.

The regulations to be: Abolition of the Government bond security, making bank notes a first lien on all the assets of the bank, including the double liability of stockholders. Introduce a guarantee fund if necessary. Limit issues to a proportion of the capital stock. Establish central redemption agencies throughout the United States. Let all notes be printed by the Government, as at present.

We would then have a currency; secure—uniform—convertible into specie—and thoroughly elastic.

Commercial prosperity would come to stay, and the Dollar of the United States, instead of the Pound Sterling, would rule the world.

SHOULD THE GOVERNMENT
RETIRE FROM BANKING ? *

" The government note, a bad, unsound, untrustworthy
currency, persecutes society at every turn and brings loss on
all but gamblers. . . . Not an hour should be lost by any
legislature who has any knowledge of the nature and working
of money to arrest the plague and sweep away inconvertible
money."—BONAMY PRICE.

THE popular opinion, now widely expressed
in intelligent quarters, that the United
States Government should go out of the banking business, is based upon the fact that one of
the important functions of banking has been as-
sumed and practically monopolized by an institution totally unfit for its performance.

The term bank, as used here, should be distinguished from the term banker. Prejudiced
writers constantly confound the two. A bank
is an extremely essential part of the business
structure. The capital stock of a bank, furnished generally by hundreds of people, the
majority of whom are in moderate circumstances, is a small proportion of the whole.

* Appeared originally in *The Forum* for February, 1895.
Printed by permission of the editor of *The Forum*.

The most important element is the deposits, which are contributed by a large part of the community. In respect to deposits, then, the people are the bank. The banker, as generally understood, is the paid officer who looks after the interests of the entire institution. Banking profits are not proportionately large, and go to the stockholders, who are again the people. Private bankers with capital of their own are comparatively few in number and cut but a small figure in the United States as compared with incorporated stock banks. These private bankers issue no notes, and are not benefited or affected directly by laws relating to banks. Laws which injure the banks do harm to the whole community; whereas laws which contribute to the proper working and prosperity of the banks help radically the whole people, especially those who depend upon daily labor for their wages.

The business of banking may be divided into three principal operations: (1) The receiving of money on deposit; (2) the loaning of the same on security of collateral or names; (3) the issuing of notes for circulation. In speaking of the United States Government being in the banking business, reference is made only to the latter feature, the note-issuing part of the business. The currency troubles in the United States are mainly due to the assumption by the Government of this prerogative, which as properly belongs, under certain restrictions, to individual associations as does the right to manufacture the necessities of life. That is to say, the experience of generations of trading people has demonstrated that the Government from its very nature, is as unfit to issue the circulating medium required by commerce as would be the faculty of a young ladies' seminary to conduct a great war.

We hear frequently the natural inquiry, Why should the banks issue currency? Why cannot a great government, with unlimited resources as a background for taxation, best maintain this instrument which affects the daily life of all the people? The answer is that currency is one of the tools of trade; and, whether good or bad, it is controlled or acted upon by the laws of trade, which are as immutable and as powerful as are any of the great laws of nature. Proud kings and powerful states have endeavored to pervert these laws by creating something out of nothing, and to wrest to themselves the benefits which are the reward of industry alone and which belong to the whole people; but, in every instance, these great laws have in the end, long confined by false conditions, broken away with the force of bursting cyclones, leaving behind them death, destruction, and ruin.

Money is one of the tools of trade, but in all banking transactions, for instance in the United States, metallic and paper money are used only to the extent of about six per cent. of the whole. How is the place of money taken as to the other ninety-four per cent.? It is made up of checks on banks, bank drafts, and other like instruments of exchange. The business of the United States, then, is done to this great percentage by bank machinery, which has grown to its present perfection as a result of the operations and development of commerce through the ages. The bank is as much the machine of trade as money is its tool. If this machinery did not exist, it would make necessary the use of actual money in every transaction. This great business is done with immense economy by banks, safely, smoothly, and in fabulous amounts. Actual coin is used to an extent of about $1\frac{1}{2}$ per cent., paper money to about $4\frac{1}{2}$ per cent., but the other 94 per cent. is just as much in effect money as if it were actually coin. Let us call it check-money, if you please. The check-money, then, is used for the larger transactions, and paper money and coin for the smaller.

Now, what is the difference between check-money and bank-notes? The first is an order of the depositor on the bank to pay a larger

sum, the second is an order of the bank on
itself to pay a smaller sum ; in effect, there is
no difference. One is payable to order, the
other to bearer ; one is as safe as the other, as
convenient and as justifiable. Commerce is to-
day using check-money to an extent of 94 per
cent. out of 100 per cent. of its transactions.
Is there any objection to giving it the privilege
of using 4½ per cent. more and furnishing,
through perfect machinery adapted for the purpose by the experience of all time, all the paper
money needed ?

The bank-note, if sent in every day for redemption (as a check is) and as it should be
sent in under any proper system of bank currency, becomes identical, in almost every
respect, with the check. The validity of check-
money is based on representatives of wealth
deposited in the bank : so is that of the bank-
note issued by the bank. Check-money will be
issued to the extent that trade requires it in a
community : so will the bank-note. Check-
money will stay out only so long as it is needed
and will come back again for redemption from
other banks who want the money : so will the
bank-note, under the daily redemption arrangement which is essential. Check-money circu-
lates in the neighborhood where it is needed :
so will the bank-note, if redeemed daily.

The increase in the number of bank-notes is regulated thus by the requirements of trade and the desire of the banks to get them out, because of the profit there is in the operation. Their decrease is effected by the pressure brought to bear by other banks, who, striving to force their own notes out, send the notes of other banks in, and the total amount kept out can thus never be more than trade actually requires. The regulation of volume is automatic. We see thus the uses, the convenience, the essential propriety of notes issued by banks.

Does the Government, usurping this function of the bank in going into the banking business to the extent of note-issuing, fulfil, with its paper issues, the mission of the bank-note? Emphatically no. The Government is made up of representatives of the people, not chosen for any peculiar business qualification, but on account of a variety of attainments, in most cases political. Now the currency has essentially to do with business—with commerce—and the regulation of it must be thoroughly in accord with the needs and requirements of trade. True, we have many students of finance and practical financiers in our own Congress. I venture to say that the Committee of the House on Banking and Currency is one of the best-informed bodies of men on financial subjects to be found in any government. They are thoroughly cognizant as to what *should* be done ; but partisan pressure, expediency, the wishes of constituents, weigh heavily. Most of all comes to them the question, What will pass? Can this or that, no matter how good, be put through? The fact stands that one bad man, or a few ignorant or vicious legislators, are enabled to block the whole body of Congress ; and at just the point when prompt and sound action is imperative they stand in the way, with the whole country in peril. We had such a state of things in the criminal tardiness of the silver-purchase repeal. Given a body like this, subject, too, to change from period to period, so that a wave of Populism and Anarchy may at any time cast up temporarily an unreasonable and dangerous representation, we turn over to them the privilege of issue—the very life-blood of trade and commerce. In addition to the dangerous element, we have the Representative who is impelled by the demands of honest but ignorant constituents. Except he be a born statesman, he necessarily sinks to the level of the voters who elected him.

There comes now a grand emergency like war, and the pressure for money is very great. There are conferences and conferences, sound council and weak council, but the easy way prevails, and the Government is authorized to create a paper currency, and the poison of fiat money enters the blood, never wholly to be eradicated. We then have the legal tender. The business of making a note-issue was thus started in this country. It has never permanently stopped since. The danger, of course, lies always in over-issue; but, with admirable firmness and decision, the limit of $400,000,000 was regarded throughout the War. But at these figures, gradually reached in an ascending scale, the greenback was productive of wild inflation, speculation in trade, extravagance in living, recklessness of expenditure, and final collapse with widespread ruin, bearing hardest upon the hand of labor. Then came slow and painful recovery. It has been computed that the War cost us eight hundred millions more than it would have cost if there had been no greenback. This is what we have already in the past to thank the greenback for.

Now let us note what follows this first warning. A cancellation of the greenback is begun. But the working poison—the deadening comfort of inoculation—stops it. Specie payments are resumed. But the eruption appears in another form : in fiat silver, the Bland dollar. No harm seems to follow, and back again we swing in the delirium of 1890 to paper. Once more the

legal tender—the Treasury note. Now the
fever is high again and we plunge with a crash
into '93, and for a second time the issues are
stopped—the second warning. But we have,
nevertheless, not stopped soon enough. We
have the over-issue. The necessity is upon us
to maintain these over-issues. From the conditions thus produced every person in the
United States is suffering more or less to-day.

The bank, issuing notes, depends upon its
business depositor to take what he needs of
them to pay out in the conduct of his business.
This puts them into circulation. No more are
taken out than business needs. Another business depositor, getting more of them than he
needs, brings them back to the bank, where
they are retired. Business thus regulates their
volume. The Government bank has no depositors and can get its notes into circulation in
no such way. It has no automatic method of
getting information as to how much money is
needed by trade, and could not act upon it if it
had. The Secretary of the Treasury, ostensible Manager of the Bank, has his hands tied.
The Government currency once out stays out;
and, as if natural conditions were not strong
enough to keep it out, the legal tenders, when
they come in for gold, must by law be paid out
again.

The tendency of an irredeemable Government currency is to drift to the money centres, and there, when its volume is too great for the uses of legitimate trade, to incite to inflation and speculation. Once at the great centres it stays there, and this is the cause of the dearth of money in the West and South. It is the real reason for that honest cry (which dishonest leaders take advantage of and fan into a dangerous flame)—the cry for more money—which ever and anon sweeps into a whirlwind, now for silver, now for State money, now for fiat money, for people's money, money on farm mortgages, money *per capita*, by the barrel, tons of it, millions and millions! I do not wonder that our Representatives from those regions which have been denuded of the natural right of a community, the right to bank-notes, feel that they must heed this cry.

There is a good honest remedy for all this. It is through the permission of note-issue to banks, without specially pledged security, under proper general supervision. We have this supervision in almost complete perfection in the national system. But the banks are now held down to an issue of 90 per cent. against par of bonds. There is no profit in this and so no relief, because banks will absolutely refuse to put out a single note voluntarily unless there

is a profit in it. The issue must eventually be
not against bond security, but against the general assets of the bank with provision for daily
redemption, so that the notes will stay to do
their work in their own neighborhood, thus
clothing them with all the advantages claimed
for State-bank issues, but with none of the
dangers.

The real want thus met, the dangerous, ignorant, but honest cry for money will cease.
Above all and before all, Government money,
the legal tenders, must be wiped out. They
are danger-breeders, inoculated with fiat poison,
clumsy, unscientific and out of place. The
Government must go out of banking, a business which it is manifestly unfitted for, and a
business which has proved disastrous to governments in every historical instance. It must
adopt once more the high and only prerogative
of a state with regard to the issue of money,
namely, the stamping upon precious metals the
state's certificate of their weight and fineness.

A WAY OUT*

PROPOSAL:

To issue $500,000,000 2½ to 3 per cent Gold Bonds ; cancel the legal tenders with proceeds thereof; allow Banks to issue currency to a percentage of 150, instead of 90 per cent., on the Bonds—total circulation to be limited by capital.

THE TREASURY BANK.

WHEN the Baltimore convention finished its work last October, it had formulated a plan for the perfecting of the banking law, mapping out the part for the banks in the work of currency reform. It did not say and did not intend to say what should be done with that great Government bank, the United States Treasury—a bank the counterpart of which exists nowhere in the world to-day; a bank with unlimited credit, which it cannot use—vast resources not available—issues out

* Before the Reform Club, New York City, December 29th, 1894. The serious dangers pointed out as threatening the Treasury at the close of the year 1894 culminated a month later, when the Government was within two days of suspension, and the country was saved from disaster only by the arrangement made with the Bond Sydicate by the President and Secretary.

of all proportions to reserves—cellars full of
hundreds of millions of useless silver—no
power to operate—with none of the privileges
of the ordinary bank or individual—paralyzed
completely on the side of executive action—
its doors wide open to the outpour of gold—
furnishing itself the legal instrument of suc-
tion, to be used over and over again to exhaust
the precious stores, but on the other hand cut
off completely from power to replenish, except
through one small antiquated aperture (the 5
per cent. bond), a crack in the wall left by
chance in the legislation of the Long Ago.
What more dreary financial spectacle than
this? What more ridiculous, if it were not so
serious?

I hesitate even to give full expression in
public as to how serious this condition, in my
opinion, seems to be. To-day the Government is receiving practically no gold at its
customs. At its one source of supply of gold
(except the sale of bonds), the percentage of
gold received is so small that it cannot be
estimated. Silver has possession of the field
of circulation ; there is absolutely no resource,
except another issue of bonds. And what
does it all mean? The people love the Greenbacks, say the congressmen ; they do not want
to fund it in bonds, because it would cost

interest to carry bonds, whereas, now it costs nothing. Nothing, say you? The interest for one year on the whole $500,000,000 would be but $10,000,000 to $15,000,000, and already, in less than a year, the Greenback has cost the people two issues of bonds of $50,000,000 each, one hundred millions instead of fifteen, with every prospect of another $50,000,000 in three months, if something is not done; to say nothing of the incalculable millions lost in the great panic of 1893.

We are facing a great problem in this country to-day. We are facing the problem of maintaining a vast mass of fiat money and fiat coin at par with the money of the world—with gold. We are facing this problem loaded with $600,000,000 of silver, with income nearly all payable in silver, with 500,000,000 of demand notes payable in gold, knocking daily at the treasury doors.

Do you wonder that the other nations of the world look askance at us and wonder whether we will or will not win in this great fight, and while they look they keep their hands well on to their own gold and well off our investments, waiting, waiting, to see what the outcome will be?

And, too, our own people are possessed with the idea of danger. Millions of dollars of cash balances are on deposit in our banks, kept there by capitalists and merchants who will not let them out in legitimate enterprises and investments until this question is permanently settled. Many wage-earners are thus kept idle and want waits at the door with winter.

NECESSITY FOR ACTION.

The Baltimore convention stirred up the banks and business men to the need of reform in the banking law. The messages of the President and Secretary have aroused the people to the condition of the Treasury and to the need of action. Immediately following this came the hearing before the committee on banking and currency, reports of which were widely circulated, and then the presentation of the Carlisle bill, the discussion in the House, and the submission of the substitute bill. All this has done great good. The advanced position taken by the President and the Secretary as to bank-note systems has been of incalculable value in the education of the people of this country, and even Congress, the fair and thinking part of it at least, has come to feel and admit that two things must be done:

First, that the legal tenders must in some manner be gotten out of the way.

Second, that their place must be taken by bank-notes.

OBJECTIONS TO PRESENT BILLS.

The debate in the House has crystallized on these lines, and the principal objections at this time to the Carlisle substitute bill are: (1) The absence of a definite provision for the retirement of the Greenback and Treasury notes. (2) The admission of state bank issues—a disturbing feature, experimental, unwise, and possibly dangerous.

OTHER OBJECTIONS.

I say principal objections. I propose to-night to note briefly some of the other objections to all plans so far advanced, and finally to make a suggestion for your consideration, which, while it will not, if adopted, accomplish at once the full requirements of currency reform, nor place us upon the sound foundation toward which it trends, will obviate the difficulties in the way of the harmonious settlement of the question for the present, and pave the way for a further completion and perfection of the system of bank-note issues based upon general security.

If the problem were simply the retirement of the legal tenders, the business men North, South, East, and West, could be aroused to the dire necessity for this action, and by urging upon Congress an issue of bonds and cancellation of paper, that body could, I believe, be prevailed upon to take this step. But, as you know, the wiping out of five hundred millions of circulation would produce a very inconvenient and possibly dangerous contraction, even though we now have too much paper out.

If the problem were simply to reform the banking system, we have the progress in education already made, the impetus given by the administration in the direction of the fundamentally correct system of bank-notes against assets, against general security with safety fund, and the solid good sense of the voters and most of their representatives, which would permit of reform solely on the lines of the tried and true national banking organization. But these two problems confront us together, and neither the Carlisle substitute bill nor the Baltimore plan—and these are practically the only plans before the country to-day—provides effectually for both problems.

It is urged by those who desire no change whatever that the national bank-notes are good enough. They are absolutely secure, convertible, uniform. Elasticity is wanting, but it is claimed that the people are satisfied, the national bank-note is as good as gold anywhere in the United States, etc., etc. It is further urged as against the new plans that they necessitate a surrender of the present national circulation of over $200,000,000 in bonds. This would throw upon the market a lot of government securities at a time when all disturbances are at least disquieting; at a time when government credit should be handled with discretion. It is true that the Carlisle substitute gives opportunity for continuation of the bond circulation, but in view of the no-profit under bonds as against the decided profit of the new circulation, the effect would probably be the same; the bonds would be sold.

Further, under the Carlisle substitute, it was urged in the House debate that there would be the old and the new national notes, the old ($206,000,000) secured by 130 per cent., and the new secured by 30 per cent. (Greenbacks). Here would be introduced a feature heterogeneous and unsatisfactory.

The advocates of the currency against assets, against general security, under the new plan, claim that the other side discuss this question as though the present system could last forever, when, as Mr. White says, there is not a national bond in existence to-day that has more than twelve years to run. The project of issuing special bonds for the purpose of maintaining a basis for bank-notes, keeping the nation in debt on that account, is contrary to all rules of common sense and good financiering, and the business men and the people would not accept it. Something, some time, and not so very far off, has got to be done in the way of giving up bond security. The change has got to be made, and why not make it now? The choice to be made at any rate in a very few years is not between the present bond plan and a plan against general assets, but between one or other of the asset plans, whether the Carlisle plan, the Baltimore plan, or something of the same kind based upon general security instead of special bond security. It will be noted that the condition of the Treasury is not met by either side in the above argument.

PROPOSAL.

The suggestions to which I referred a few moments ago in the interest of harmonious adjustment, and more especially in the interest of the Treasury, which, in my mind, is an interest far beyond any present requirements of the bank system, except as that system can aid in placing our national finances on a sure basis, is as follows:

Issue $500,000,000 of low-rate bonds, $2\frac{1}{2}$ per cent. to 3 per cent., payable in gold and payable at the option of the government. Bonds to be delivered $200,000,000 now, $100,000,000 in six months, $100,000,000 in twelve months, $100,000,000 in eighteen months ; but all to be subscribed for now, under forfeit.

Cancel legal tenders with the proceeds of these bonds.

Continue the national bank issues and system exactly as at present, except that banks be allowed to take out circulation to the extent of 150 per cent. on bonds instead of 90 per cent., as at present ; circulation to be limited to amount of capital ; notes still to be a first lien upon assets and double liability of stockholders. Establish a safety fund replenishable when impaired, continue government guarantee and, for the present, government redemption for a very short period, with the idea in a few months of establishing daily redemption. The emergency circulation feature of the Baltimore plan could, too, be adopted if deemed wise in connection with this proposition.

SMOOTH SAILING.

Let everything go on as before, safely, uniformly, with the same provision for convertibility and a new provision to a percentage, for elasticity with general security (which is really absolute security) back of it.

We make thus a conservative, well-guarded step towards the plan of issue against general security without bonds, to which we must ultimately come as the only sound solution in the end, but we retain temporarily two-thirds of the bond security and obtain with the other third a measure of elasticity sufficient for the present. It may be noted here that the Carlisle plan furnishes a proportion of elastic issue equal to 52½ per cent. of capital, the Baltimore plan 50 per cent. thereof, and the suggestion here made, 33⅓ per cent. of same.

Stated periods could and should be adopted for the further retirement of bond security and permissible increase of elastic issue. The public are enabled so to test the security and, as it were, to become accustomed to a new and the only right principle, without letting go altogether of old-time anchorage to bonds. The dangerous indebtedness of the government is thus speedily wiped out. The bonds once subscribed for become a bulwark of security to the national credit, and the act restores immediately the confidence of the great foreign investment contingent, a confidence which has been so fast slipping away from us, and which is so important an element in our general prosperity. Gold will begin to flow our way. Confidence restored, our own people will renew investments and put out enterprise. The sure foundation so sadly needed will have been begun to be laid.

As to the national currency, as I have said, it stays. The two hundred millions already out stay out. Additional circulation on the same bonds is added as the Greenbacks retire and the need is felt. There are no new notes with 30 per cent. security and old ones with 130. Each is as good in the pocket as under the magnifying-glass. No minute inspection is necessary to see what is what. The public, the innocent bill-holders, go right on taking in and paying out, just as well protected, absolutely undisturbed, safe and tranquil, with the bank-bill in the wallet, meantime that a mighty reform is taking place in the currency, as silent and as momentous as the vast but imperceptible changes wrought by chemistry in the bowels of the earth.

Without yielding one point as to what is the only sound principle of bank issues, namely, that they should be against general security, the total assets of the bank, the short bills receivable, the representatives of products, the results of toil, the promissory notes of hundreds of thousands of honest promisers who will keep their promises and pay their notes, working day and night to do so, as they did in 1893, and have done in every year before and since— without yielding one point as to the doctrine that this is and must be the only true and ultimate outcome of currency reform in this coun-

try—I venture to put out this proposition as a
step in the direction towards which we are
heading, a step which must be followed by
others, but, above all, a step which clears away
the danger and closes up the Treasury Bank
and takes care of the national credit, which to
me, as I have said, is an interest far above the
question of the best thing for the banks as
banks. For the bankers of this country, I am
thoroughly convinced, are citizens of the
United States first and bankers afterwards.

MR. CORNWELL'S CURRENCY PLAN.

(The *New York Times*, Editorial, December 31st, 1894.)

It seems pretty plain that in this part of the country the
opinion of business men very generally is concentrating upon
two points in the financial situation—the final retirement of
the greenbacks and their replacement by national bank notes,
issued on the bonds with which the greenbacks are retired.
The suggestions of Mr. W. C. Cornwell, President of the
New York State Bankers' Association, which we published
yesterday morning, have some new features that are well worth
attention. Mr. Cornwell's plan is intended not merely to meet
the present difficulty—grave as that is—but, while doing so,
to provide for a gradual transition to a sound and lasting and
elastic credit currency. With this end in view, he proposes
an issue of $500,000,000 in low-term bonds, to be subscribed
now, but to be issued in installments extending over eighteen
months, payable at the discretion of the government. On
these bonds he proposes to allow the issue of bank-notes to
the amount of 150 per cent. of the bonds deposited, to be secured by a guarantee fund, by a first lien on all assets and by
the personal liability of shareholders, the issues of each bank

to be limited by its capital. He further suggests that the emergency-issue feature of the Baltimore plan could be adopted, if desirable.

Under this plan, as the government should be in a position to redeem the bonds, the sufficiency of the safety fund and the general liens would be tested, and the banks could gradually proceed on that basis. There is no serious question that the provisions of the Baltimore plan would in practice be found to afford ample security ; the principal objection to its adoption has been the fact that the public might not recognize the safety of the notes and that unnecessary disturbance might ensue. Mr. Cornwell's plan meets this objection by the provision for the continuance for a time of the bond security and also by a temporary redemption by the Government. It is probable that no new scheme could be worked with entire smoothness and security without this feature. Ultimately the banks should be required to redeem their own notes, and some provision should be made for their regular presentation for redemption. But it is of the last importance that any change in the currency should not breed the faintest distrust, and this can probably be secured only by temporary Government redemption.

It will be noticed that Mr. Cornwell's plan is one in which the advocates of the Baltimore plan and those of the Carlisle plan can find some of their own most important provisions. It differs from both in aiming at a gradual but thorough withdrawal of the legal-tender notes ; which are the only source of real difficulty and danger. We are very much mistaken if the discussion of the past month has not convinced the country that no plan will be of real and permanent advantage that does not get rid of the legal tenders. No amount of gold in the Treasury can surely suffice for the prompt redemption of notes perpetually reissued and liable constantly to return for redemption. Mr. Cornwell's plan has the great merit of being the first that embraces the essentials of a sound system of bank currency, ultimately independent of the Government, and, with this, the sure disposal of the legal-tender notes.

THE GOLD STANDARD

AN ARGUMENT IN FAVOR OF A SINGLE STAND-ARD OF GOLD—THE BEST OF METALS NONE TOO GOOD FOR AMERICANS.*

MR. PRESIDENT and gentlemen of the Liberal Club: There are in operation throughout the universe and co-incident with the community of man, certain great laws which are as unerring in their workings as the laws of Nature herself, and no decree of man or State can swerve them from their relentless course. Recognized by man, given full sway, and with human laws conformed completely to them, they become the gentle friend even the abject slave of man. But thwarted, with-stood, or met with dissembling action, they become cyclone breeders of disaster and blood-shed.

These are the laws of Trade and Commerce.

Let the puny Populist, raising his sacri-legious hands pipe out " Let there be money,"

* Before the Liberal Club, Buffalo, N. Y., February 16, 1894, in reply to Gen. Francis A. Walker, on Bimetallism.

and they will grind him to powder and scatter him with the wind-swept dust of his Western prairie.

Let the Assignat-maker of France turn loose his worthless decree-sustained paper money, and these laws will wipe out his tribe with the flames and blood of a Revolution.

Distress and disaster follow in the wake of Commerce's laws broken—mellow prosperity ripens under their sunshine, if profoundly kept.

It is no wonder then that we turn with much interest to see what history records as to the action of these laws regarding the Standard of Value, and we find that Commerce in every age has decided what shall be the Standard.

The decision in this century is for Gold.

England, the United States, Germany, Belgium, and Holland, Austria, and Russia have recorded this decision. Says the report of the Special Commission of the Austrian Upper House in 1879 : " It had become clear as long ago as the decade of 1860 to 1870, when Europe was becoming saturated with gold, that this was the only metal fitted to be the standard of nations of advanced civilization." " Gold was dominant and the standard of value," says this report, " in all trade on a great scale, as early as the 14th and 15th centuries, even though silver was then the standard in all domestic

exchange. . . . In every age there is some
metal dominant in the industry of the world,
which forces its way with elemental strength
in the face of any public regulation, and in our
day, gold is that metal."

Why has this decision been made?

Because Commerce insists on the best medium for its own requirements.

Commerce in this last century has needed
a metal, precious, but still of sufficient quantity to be used as an everyday medium of
exchange—fusible, ductile, malleable, easily
divisible, indestructible, or nearly so, and of
vast purchasing power, concentrated in small
bulk.

Has silver these qualities?

It is fusible, ductile, malleable, divisible, not
so easily so as gold, but sufficiently.   It is
practically durable, not so nearly indestructible
as gold, but nearly enough.

Has it vast purchasing power concentrated
in small bulk.

No.

For that reason the vast increase in commerce in the last century, the enormous size of
its transactions, the resistless drawing together
of the great commercial world, through the
discovery, subjugation, and application of the
great powers of nature—steam and electricity

—almost annihilating time and space—these things have made it necessary for commerce to select for its transactions a metal which, while possessing all other requirements, shall have in a pre-eminent degree this one quality of concentrated value.

Silver has not vast purchasing power concentrated in small bulk.

During the deliberations of the Brussels Conference, M. Rothschild, delegate for Great Britain, says :

" Our firm have, on several occasions, been obliged to send a million sterling in sovereigns or bar gold abroad, which million, when packed up, amounts to a weight of about 10 tons. Is it likely, and even if desirable, would it be feasible and practical, supposing a ratio of 20 to 1 were established, to send 200 tons of metal at one and the same time ? It seems to me that the operation would be impossible, and the sender would, therefore, naturally elect or rather be compelled to send gold, even if it had to be bought at a premium."

It is the old law of natural selection and survival of the fittest, and, for the same reason that in turn iron, lead, tin, and copper were dropped, so silver has fallen out of place in international commerce.

And yet it is a beautiful metal ; so surpassingly brilliant, says our distinguished guest here to-night, in one of the standard works which have made his name known wherever money is made a study of, "so surpassingly brilliant, that it almost justifies the preference expressed by the barefoot boy of Sir Walter Scott, ' Give me the white money, please.' "

The barefoot boy of commerce of the old centuries has grown to be an enormous giant in these latter days. He has perhaps lost his gentle manners, for now, when he is offered the white money, he thunders out the demand " Give me gold," and he speaks in English, German, French, Hungarian, and a lot of other languages, and he does n't say " please."

I do not think the bimetallists anywhere deny the superiority of gold for the purposes of the commerce of to-day.

I have quoted from one of the works of Mr. Walker. He says further in his volume on money :

" The extreme beauty of silver, brightest of all the metals, together with its numerous applications in the economy of life, make it an object of admiration and desire among peoples in all degrees of social advancement. Easily fusible, highly ductile, practically imperishable, silver would have filled our utmost conception of a money metal had not the earth yielded *one transcendent product in comparison with which even silver fades from desire.*"

That product is gold, and of gold Mr. Walker says : " Its compendious value allows a vast amount of purchasing power to be concentrated for conveyance or for concealment in little bulk. A small planchet of gold has the power to command the labor of days. But while thus precious it is found in sufficient quantity to allow of its convenient use as an every-day medium of exchange. Its durability, fusibility, ductility, and malleability form a group of properties of the highest importance for the purposes of coinage and circulation."

The choice of the world then is Gold.

It is even the choice of the bimetallists themselves, except for one thing.

At the Brussels Conference, Mr. Van den Berg, delegate of the Netherlands, one of the strongest bimetallists present, said :

"From whatever side I look at the question I always come back to the dilemma, Is universal monometallism possible and practicable ; yes or no? If yes, if it can be demonstrated that there is no lack of gold for the monetary needs of the whole world, I become a turncoat—allow me the word—a turncoat, and place myself beside my present antagonists."

The question, then, it seems to me, narrows itself down to whether or no there is, and will be, enough gold.

I desire for a moment to leave the question there and briefly to cite some of the principal objections to bimetallism.

GOVERNMENT INTERFERENCE.

And first as to the interference of governments which would be necessary in the adopt-

7

ion of international bimetallism. What are the functions of a government with respect to standard money; what ought it to attempt and what can it properly effect?

The best thought of the nineteenth century, among unprejudiced economists, approves of as little interference by governments as is at all possible in the affairs of commerce. We have had some sad examples in this country of the disasters which follow upon a violation of this principle. Our own silver bubble, which had been filling with wind since 1878, has burst at last, leaving blighted hopes and empty factories and hunger and cold instead of the soapy rainbows that our inflationist statesmen so loved to look upon. And these windy criminals are still mussing around in the suds endeavoring to blow up seigniorage and other silver bubbles.

It has even been suggested by so high an authority as Herbert Spencer, that the very Government stamping of coin attesting weight and fineness might be dispensed with, leaving the question of a medium and the attestation of it to commerce itself. But admitting that the stamping of metal to give guaranty of weight and quality is a proper function, the declaration of legal tenders is the second assumption of authority by a government. This establishes what shall be received by the Government itself for taxes and what a contract made in money shall be paid in, avoiding thus any misunderstandings or contentions. But Mr. Robert Giffin says: " Even without a declaration of legal tender, metallic currency if a good one would circulate and be useful much to the same extent as it does now." But the bimetallist contends that the Government must keep a stable standard, from period to period, keeping both metals in use either by fixing the ratio forcibly or by changing it every time it is necessary. And in the course of all this it would be necessary for the government to insist that all contracts must be fulfilled in gold or silver at the certain ratio. No other contracts in money could be permitted, or bimetallism would become of no value. The freedom of the individual must be restricted. Emergencies would arise, as in case of war, where large sums of gold would be required; very complicated questions would have to be dealt with—questions on which even experts are not agreed. The question is, even if it were worth the trouble, Could governments be depended upon to regulate such problems? Governments! What are they? Tribunals full of people who have no intellectual interest in financial subjects; no quali-

fication of any sort or kind for dealing with
them, themselves elected by constituencies still
more unfit, with little conception of the value
of the problems, and no means whatsoever of
forming practical conclusions.

Let me say one thing further: if you read
carefully the deliberations of the Brussels Conference, the very last international expression
on this subject, you will be thoroughly convinced of the impossibility of getting governments together on bimetallism. The positive
refusals of the gold-standard nations to even
consider international bimetallism places the
matter entirely out of reach. I do not say we
cannot come to a more extended international
subsidiary use of silver on a gold basis, but to
get governments to act together on the complicated questions which would surely arise
under a managed currency—a currency artifi-
cially controlled by politics and not automatic
under the great undeviating laws of commerce
—to do this will be surely impossible.

EXPERIENCE OF FRANCE.

And now as to the experience of France.
It is claimed as a principal argument by the
bimetallists that France, from 1803 to 1873,
under the free coinage of both gold and silver,
was for seventy years successfully bimetallic

at a legal ratio of 15½ of silver to one of gold. To this the monometallist replies that in order to be truly bimetallic gold and silver in a country must be used indifferently as a legal tender. Carefully prepared tables show that from 1803 to 1873 either one metal or the other was at so serious a premium that they could not possibly pass as equivalents. At a premium of from one to two per cent. no man would think of paying a debt of $500 in a metal that would cost him $505 or $510 to procure. And that was almost continuously the condition, and at times the variations were very much wider, running as high as 7½ per cent. in two instances. For instance, in 1813, 16.25 to 1, and in 1814, 15.04 to 1 ; or 7½ per cent. variation, and about the same difference in 1819 and 1820.

In 1850 came the immense gold finds of California and Australia. Up to that time France, since 1803, had been practically on the silver standard, and gold was at a premium except in a very few years, at from 1 to 2 per cent. From 1850 on, France went to the gold standard and stayed there until 1867. Then the great change began again—until in 1874 she must suspend the free coinage of silver or go over absolutely to the silver standard. She suspended it and to-day is on what is called the "limping standard."

The conclusions are that France was never truly bimetallic.

As to the steadiness of the market ratio between gold and silver and its being kept so on account of French bimetallism its opponents claim that the steadiness was natural, that similar periods of steadiness have occurred before and that as to immense finds of gold in 1850 and after, the fact that gold did not materially fall in value was due not to the French ratio but to gold being really the choice of commerce, and that the influx was received with joy and quickly absorbed by the commercial world.

FALL OF PRICES.

Now as to the fall in prices brought about by scarcity of gold the monometallists claim that in the last fifteen years gold prices have fallen 20 per cent. while silver prices have remained unchanged. If then the two had been linked together, the fall would have been one-half, that is 10 per cent. If, in other words, we had had international bimetallism, there would anyway have been a fall in prices of 10 per cent. in the last fifteen years. The evil then (and it is claimed by some that it is not an evil) of falling prices could not have been prevented. This evil will go on anyway say probably to the extent of 10 per cent. in fifteen years, and it must be met. Great gold discoveries or great extension of bank paper temporarily prevent, but the fall afterwards continues, and bimetallism cannot stop it.

There is, however, quite a ray of hope, as I shall afterwards show, in the increase in gold production in the last two years.

There is a great deal of talk about the distressed condition of the world ascribed to fall of prices and used by the bimetallist as a grand argument, but Mr. David A. Wells, that most distinguished economist, accounts for the fall in price of all staple articles of commerce which really have fallen during the last twenty years by the economy of production and economy of transportation, and Mr. Horace White says:

" He has not grouped them altogether as our bimetallist friends commonly do, but he has taken each one separately."

Mr. Atkinson also says:

" The gold standard's great and complete justification in this country is to be found in the fact that since specie payment was re-established upon the gold unit of value on the 1st of January, 1879, there has been a progressive and almost continuous reduction in the price of the necessaries of life, accompanied by such improvements due to science and invention in their production, that there is not a single important article that can be named of which the reduction in price is not more than justified by the reduction in cost due to labor-saving improvements which have been applied either to primary or secondary production and to distribution since that date or since 1873. On the other hand, the lawful unit of value, a gold dollar, is completely justified by the benefit, which has ensued from its adoption, to that great majority of the working people of this country who earn their daily bread from salaries, earnings or wages. There was never a period in the history of the world in which an industrious workman of this country, possessing skill and aptitude in the higher or lower grades of labor, could secure so many units of gold in compensation for his work as during the years 1890, 1891, and a part of 1892 ; nor has there been a period in which he could buy so large a quantity of the necessaries of life with his earnings as in the year 1891 and the early part of 1892."

Mr. White referring to the alleged conspiracy against the debtor class, says :

"What is meant by ' debtor class ' in this discussion ? All men who are not bankrupt are both creditors and debtors. The fact that they are not bankrupt implies that they have more due to them in one way and another than they owe. I am proud to believe that the vast majority of my countrymen are of this class, *i.e.*, of the creditor class. I take it that we are not legislating specially for bankrupts. Certainly it would not be wise to change our standard of value for their accommodation. Such a change would produce a great many new bankrupts and would not save any old ones."

Mr. White replying to the argument that national and State debts are enhanced by the gold standard, wants to know why the standard of value for all the countless daily business transactions should be changed simply to meet this point, when the clearings for one week in the United States amount to about $1,100,000,-

ooo which is about double the interest-bearing debt of the nation. He says :

" Add to this the payment of wages and the retail transactions not embraced in the clearings and multiply it by the fifty-two weeks of the year and you will see how large a cannon you are loading to kill a mosquito and what a tremendous recoil it must have."

THE SUPPLY OF GOLD.

I would like now to turn back to the conclusion reached in the early part of this address, namely, that the question has narrowed down to whether or not there is or will be gold enough for the gold standard. On this point a recent article on the production of gold throws pertinent and most encouraging light.

It is shown that the gold production in 1892 was 138,000,000 which is more than the average of the great years from 1850 to 1860. That the production for 1893 will probably show 150,-000,000, an increase even over 1892. That this increase comes largely from the recently discovered South African gold fields, that they may be expected to constantly increase, and will probably not reach their maximum figures for the next thirty years. Those who know the country well think that there is a gold field in the Transvaal that will not be exhausted for centuries, and that the output now ranging between 20,000,000 and 30,000,000 will be in-

creased in three or four years to 50,000,000,
and this can be kept up for a generation from
those mines alone which are now being worked.
What with new processes enabling ore containing only $2 in gold a ton to be worked profit-
ably, and a steady increase guaranteed from
Africa, Mr. Fraenkel, the author of the article,
concludes : " It is not impossible that in a few
years a quantity of gold not far from 100,000,000
will be available for monetary use. If this should
prove true, it would seem futile to speak of an
impending scarcity of gold."

A few words about the commercial condition
of the United States in this matter and I am
done ; and in what I am to say now I shall
use, very materially condensed, the demonstra-
tion of Mr. Edward Atkinson.

GOLD BEST FOR THE UNITED STATES.

The whole world is becoming one neighborhood, and with this, each country tends to
increase the excess of production in which it
excels every other. Those products of which
the production pays the highest wages at the
lowest cost of production will be the ones in
which any country can most successfully com-
pete.

The United States can, on these conditions,
produce, far in excess of all our wants, all the

necessaries of life. Fuel, food, timber, and metals are the things that we excel in on conditions of highest wages and lowest cost of production. Now, the nations producing fuel, metal, and timber on these conditions are thereby enabled to apply labor-saving machinery to other branches of production most advantageously, and the machine-using nations of the world control its commerce. On the fuel, food, timber, and metal basis, then, the United States controls the commerce of the world.

The commerce of Great Britain and the United States with each other is greater than with any other nation or State. They are the two principal importing and exporting countries. They are also the two chief machine-using nations of the world, and consequently practically dictate terms and conditions for all other international commerce.

And what are these terms as regards the fulfillment of contracts? They are for their discharge in comparison with the unit of gold. It is called pound sterling, but it is actually 113 grains of gold. Why has this been chosen? Let me give Mr. Atkinson's own words:

" Because the unit of gold is the safest, surest, least costly, and most convenient standard and method of determining the relation of one commodity to others, in the exchange of which

commerce consists. If it had not been the safest and best
unit some other would have been discovered and adopted.
This unit or standard of value has been slowly developed as
an international measure in the progress of mankind without
regard to legislation of any kind, and without the interven-
tion or interference of any act of legal tender.

Bimetallism seeks to establish some other
unit or standard—an international legal tender
of gold and silver. Do you imagine for one
minute that commerce would accept it? You
might wipe out the pound sterling, but international commerce would spurn the new tender
and make one of its own. It would cling to
gold ; a certain number of grains of it, say one
hundred, and that would be commerce's reply
to infringement of her laws. And if you went
still further and forbade its use, woe be to the
meddlers who thus tamper with the imperial
laws of all time, laws that in the back centuries
have swept away kings and principalities and
kingdoms under like aggravation.

This country is the greatest creditor nation
of the world. The articles we buy from others
we can spare. The articles they buy from us
they must have. The price of these things has
been established in gold, and when we want
gold (more than we want other goods) gold we
can have. Shall we throw away this advantage ? Under bimetallism our hands would be

tied. We would have to accept silver. Have
you any doubt that the other nations would
pay us in silver? And when the experience
of the ages, the maturity of all time, and six
centuries of a gradually developed choice have
decreed gold to be the most valuable, shall we
accept the baser metal?

But, says the bimetallist, there will then be
no baser metal. One will be as good as the
other. Yes, by declaration of the earthly powers, but can royal edict turn stones to bread or
stay by proclamation the ocean's restless tide?
Shall we depend upon the assurances of an
untried theory which overwhelmingly broke
to pieces in 1873, and so depending, take the
chances of loss and great disaster?

The misery and distress of falling prices appeal to us; but although the bewildered Dane
charged it to cowardice, we of commerce would
" rather bear the ills we have than fly to others
that we know not of."

Let us by private and public charity do all
we can to relieve the world's distress ; but here
in this favored land let us accept open-handed
the golden prosperity which commerce is ready
to pour down to us, firmly convinced that
gold, the best ! the best ! is none too good for
Americans.

INTERNATIONAL BIMETALLISM NEITHER PRACTICAL NOR DESIRABLE *

THE BIMETALLIC PICTURE.

THE picture drawn for our consideration by the bimetallists is a most interesting one. They depict, first of all, the distress prevailing in the world since 1873, when they say the machinations of the enemies of silver, the selfish efforts of gold-loving tyrants broke down a perfect system of bimetallism which had prevailed with almost flawless perfection for seventy years. They picture since then the terrible strain caused by an insufficient gold supply; the fatal fall of prices consequent upon it; the crowding out of business enterprise; the pall of ruin settling over everything. After depicting all this with graphic pencil, they call upon the nations to combine, to touch with magic wand the vast hoards of silver, and, turning them to gold, to open the flood-gates and let in this glorious stream upon the commerce of

* Before the Commercial Club, Chicago, April 28th, 1894.

the world, raising prices, equalizing exchange between all the nations, steadying the money mass to such an extent that international trade will be fructified to the last extremity, to the betterment of every soul on the broad earth ; until each inhabitant thereof shall thrive and wax fat in the sunshine of Universal Prosperity.

This is the dream of our bimetallic friends. So rosy, so full of comfort, so philanthropic, so plausible ; alas ! so near to apparent reason, that one is loth to search for error, feeling that if this is not the truth, it ought to be.

And yet we must turn to the practicable and desirable, and coldly weigh facts, first for the world, and then for ourselves—and that is what we are here for to-night.

I am sorry that the bimetallists have chosen a time for agitating this subject when the whole industrial system in the United States has been prostrated by panic brought on by a senseless, long-continued, obstinate pursuit of the silver will-o'-the-wisp in this country. Their allusions, at this time, to distress in the business world receive, consequently, considerable atten-tion although the fact is, the present depression is *not* an element of their argument. It is also unfortunate at this time, when we have suffered so much from silver agitation, and had so well-nigh blocked it by the Silver Purchase Repeal, that the matter is once more stirred up and the brilliant picture of Universal Prosperity is thrown upon the midnight sky, to be gazed at by a crowd of hungry and idle people in this country. Bimetallism is thus urged, inferentially at least, as the cure-all of present ills.

How futile is the proposition, I shall endeavor to-night to point out. And with all respect to the distinguished men here and elsewhere, who honestly believe the doctrine, I am bound to say that I believe it to be as full of error as the pursuit of perpetual motion, the advocacy of fiat money, or any of the other dreams of magic which have engaged the attention of the world since Adam started out from the Garden under the ban or blessing of the inflexible rule which has prevailed ever since, namely : Labor is the price of Bread.

GOLD THE CHOICE.

The high laws of commerce, untrammelled by acts of human government, have decided from the earliest times what shall be the standard of value in international exchange. For five centuries gold has been dominant in all trade on a large scale, even though silver has been the standard in domestic exchange. And in this last century, gold has been rapidly forced to the front, so that the Austrian Commission in 1879 declared that "it had become clear as long ago as the decade of 1860 to 1870, when Europe was becoming saturated with gold, that this was the only metal fitted to be the standard of nations of advanced civilization.

Gold alone has in a pre-eminent degree the quality of vast purchasing power concentrated in small bulk. And gold is the choice of the world, as evinced by its adoption by the most civilized nations.

Our bimetallist friends claim with distinct manifestations of resentment that this, that, and the other leading nation, did not naturally select gold—that England stumbled into it, Germany wickedly forced herself into it—the United States was feloniously and criminally seduced into it, etc., etc. Nevertheless, the great economic truth that natural laws over-power, sooner or later, all attempts of an artificial character would long ere this have prevailed and changed the standard of gold countries, if it were not absolutely true that gold is the choice of the most advanced and civilized commerce.

M. Rothschild, the banker, said at the Brussels Conference, not more than two years ago :

" When we consider that the whole of England's commerce, and a great part of that of other countries, is carried on by bills of exchange on London, which are naturally payable in

8

gold, I think it must be admitted that the world in general transacts its business on a gold basis, and that in reality such a thing as a double standard, except in a modified form, does not exist even in those countries who profess to pay in either of the two metals.

Money for the purposes of international money, must be universally acceptable. Nobody denies that gold is so. Is silver? Ah! That is all that "ails" it! *It is not generally acceptable.* If it were, there would be no need of conferences, treaties and international agreements to make it current, to make it "go." Gold "goes" without any of this artificial machinery.

"If," says Horace White, "silver were as acceptable as gold, we would all be 'silver-bugs.'"

So one great nation after another has taken up gold, and after the most careful and deliberate consideration, has adopted it. The advance under the natural law of selection has been irrepressible, aided by the excessive and continually increasing production of silver. This alarming increase made it necessary in 1873 to suspend the free coinage of silver in bimetallic States, because of the fall in price of the metal and the ever-widening gap between the market price and the legal value in comparison with gold. The suspension, of course, increased the depreciation.

FALL OF PRICES.

The year 1873, then, markes the final abandonment of bimetallism, and the bimetallists
point to the fact that since 1873 there has
been a steady fall in prices, claimed by them
to have produced distress and ruin and to be
due to the steady appreciation of gold.

Such reliable statisticians as David A. Wells
and Edward Atkinson have carefully investi-
gated this matter and have practically laid at
rest this argument.

These gentlemen prove conclusively that
there has been no decline in the price of necessary articles of food, clothing or construction
which cannot be accounted for by a cheapening
of production or transportation—that if we go
back to 1860, before the period of inflation
caused by our own Civil War, the Franco-Prus-
sian war, the Austro-Prussian war, and all the
other great struggles of that era, if we go back to
1860,there has been no general decline whatever.
Mr. Atkinson shows that if the articles of food,
clothing, fuel, and construction required by the
average mechanic per year are grouped in
what is called a multiple standard or portion,
the workman on his wages in 1850 could have
purchased 4. 9 / 10 portions ; in 1860, 5. 1/ 10 ;
in 1865, 4.2/10 ; in 1873, the culmination of the
speculation period, he could purchase 5. 1/2

portions. From 1879 wages have been steadily advancing. In 1890 the mechanic could buy 8. 66/100 portions, and in 1891 and 1892, 9 portions. Mr. Atkinson says:

"If that is the effect of a so-called 'fatal fall' in prices, which is to be attributed to the appreciation of gold, to whom has it been fatal? Why should it be resisted! Conditions which have made the workman's life twice as easy in 1890 as in 1865, and which make him nearly twice as well off as he was in 1873, may well be maintained by him."

PROSPERITY SINCE 1873.

Since 1873, the United States has had an era of marvellous prosperity.

Under the head of "Twenty Years of Progress," Mr. Edward Atkinson shows that our population since 1873 has increased 57 per cent. Our per capita national debt has diminished 75 per cent. That the postal receipts (foremost sign of progress) have increased 218 per cent. Appropriations for public schools increased 103 per cent. Grain crop increased 96 per cent. Western farm mortgages have steadily decreased since 1880, and the farmers in many States have grown rich and are lenders themselves.

In cotton the increase has been 132 per cent. In iron, 257 per cent. In steel, from almost nothing to the leadership of the world. Tonnage of the Great Lakes 787 per cent. Last year the traffic through the Sault Ste. Marie Canal was over ten million tons, exceeding that through the Suez Canal by two million tons.

As to wheat, it cost 242 per cent. more to move a bushel of wheat from Chicago to New York in 1873 than it did in 1892, and the cost of producing wheat has been reduced in about a similar proportion.

The record of the twenty years has been one of steady progress, and from 1879, the date of the restoration of specie payment on a gold basis, one of almost undimmed prosperity.

But think, says the bimetallist, what it might have been under bimetallism. Think of the variation in exchange between the countries of the world and the consequent loss of business resulting therefrom.

THE EXAMPLE OF FRANCE.

Then the bimetallists point to France as an example of what bimetallism can do—their only argument from actual experience—claiming that France from 1803 to 1873, under the free coinage of both gold and silver, was for seventy years successfully bimetallic at a legal ratio of fifteen and a half silver to one of gold.

This is the only experiment in bimetallism that amounts to anything, and it practically fell to pieces. It fell in 1873, just as it would have fallen in 1850, if it had not been for the great gold discoveries. During all that period, from 1820 to 1850, France was practically a silver-using country.

Silver being cheaper than the legal rate, and tending to become cheaper still, had expelled gold from circulation (remember this is France for thirty years, right in the middle of the much-boasted bimetallic period)—gold, mind you, had been expelled by cheap silver until 1848 ; the Bank of France had hardly any gold left in its till. Suppose now that instead of immense gold discoveries (the only thing that saved bimetallism in 1850 from annihilation) a change had occurred, not in the direction of making the cheaper metal—silver—dearer than the other, but in the direction of making it cheaper still. There would then have been no gold to arrest the fall, France would have been powerless and would either have had to slide on to the silver standard or else close her mints, as she actually was compelled to do in 1873. To be truly bimetallic, gold and silver, in a country, must be used indifferently as a legal tender. Carefully prepared tables show that in France from 1803 to 1873 either one metal or the other was at so serious a premium that the two could not possibly pass as equivalents.

THE LATIN UNION.

As to the bimetallism of the Latin Union, the suspension of the coinage of silver, as a result of the immense fall in price, took place in this aggregation only after the channels of the various States had been stuffed full of the white metal. At the Brussels Conference it was stated that "in the countries of the Latin Union it would be impossible to force into circulation a single five-franc piece over and above those which are in use at present."

To-day the Latin Union is practically on a gold basis. The five-franc silver coins have a full debt-paying power, but only because they are tokens always exchangeable for gold at par. I cannot help quoting that graphic picture of the Union taken from the speech of the delegate of Sweden at the Conference last referred to:

"The States of the Latin Union, and especially Belgium, can tell us something of the practical side of bimetallism. Those States entered one fine day full of international confidence under the magnificent arches of a bimetallic system supported by pillars of gold and silver ranged in a pre-established harmony of fifteen and a half to one. But the harmony was disturbed, silver fell, the white pillars were transformed into walls which barred the outlet and they were imprisoned. In prison tempers are easily soured, and the Latin States no longer bless the treaty of 1865."

A TRIAL OF BIMETALLISM.

Bimetallism seeks to bring about an apparent, unnatural, ephemeral prosperity by raising prices. The effect would be merely transitory and would be followed by an inevitable reaction.

" Everybody," says a forcible writer, "everybody distrusts silver coin, of which there is evidently more than necessary. Everybody, therefore, seeks to keep his gold, and at this moment it is that everybody is asked to agree by international contract to coin the disliked silver in unlimited quantities, while remaining free to get and keep gold each as best he may."

It is sought to create a full debt-paying power for silver, which nobody wants much of in his pocket, and can only carry a moderate amount of in his safe, obliging creditors to receive *unlimited* quantities of a metal of which they can keep only a *limited* quantity.

This is certainly a flagrant violation of natural law.

The supply of silver is practically unlimited. Why not use paper? That of course would be fiat money; but silver in forcible use by legal tender declaration, intrinsically worth fifty cents on the dollar (with prospects of further depreciation under enormous production, stimulated by international bimetallism) is virtually fiat money. How can it be otherwise?

What makes the fifty-cent dollar good but the fiat, not of one government but a dozen?

The coin which is not worth as much in the melting-pot as in the pocket, is not true money.

This is the fire test of economics—put the buzzard product of bimetallism in it and smell the singeing feathers.

Well, let us see what would follow, if, after all, the nations could be made to agree and international bimetallism became a fact. The mints of the world are now practically open at the ratio of fifteen and a half to one, to the free and unlimited coinage of dollars, crowns, florins, marks, or five-franc pieces. The annual production of silver on a rapidly falling market price has risen in the last twenty years from $87,000,000 to over $200,000,000. What figures of production will not be reached if prices by bimetallic union can be maintained? The production will be stimulated tenfold. From the moment the mints are opened producers of silver will no longer be at the mercy of consumption in the arts or the demands of the silver-using countries. There will be no competition from other producers in the great markets of the world. For forty to fifty cents worth of silver bullion anyone can get a dollar coined. With smiles on their faces they will carry each his load of bullion to the mint, and, as fast as the coining presses can coin, they will carry away their bags of dollars or five-franc pieces. " It must not be overlooked that the work done by a coining-press is not in proportion to the size of a country on whose behalf it operates. Whether it be in Brussels, Paris, London, or Philadelphia, it will produce in an hour or in a day the same number of coins." And the producer, carrying away his bags-full, will have no difficulty in making them circulate. Wherever there is a debt to be paid it will be paid, by virtue of the glorious international law, in the silver-producers' hard and heavy cash, no matter what the dissatisfied creditor may say. Is there any limit to the amount of silver that would be thus discharged upon the world? The annual output, it has been estimated, would rise from $200,000,000 to $400,000,000. Where would it go? Out of the pockets and safes into the banks, and they? More and more encumbered and embarrassed with it they would seek to get rid of it ; utterly unfit as it is for large payments which the banks are expected to make. Then would come the struggle for gold. Hear what Mr. Rothschild says. He certainly is prepared to say what the great banks would do.

"We are then asked," he says, "suddenly to go back to what took place before 1873, and to forget the enormous

progress which civilization has made in facilitating the financial operations of the world.

" It is proposed to revert to a great extent to the old state
of things which existed until 1873, namely, to open all or
part of the mints of Europe to the free coinage of silver and
to discuss a ratio to be fixed.

"Well, gentlemen, have the bimetallists for a single moment thought what the result would be if such a measure is
introduced? Why, clearly from that very moment, the Bank
of England note would cease to represent sovereigns and
would be payable in depreciated currency, because the Bank
of England could never pay its notes in gold and at the same
time be purchasers of an unlimited amount of silver, for within
a very short period the twenty-five millions of gold which the
bank now holds in its vault would, in my opinion, have dis-
appeared and have become replaced by silver.

" In the final adjustment of international balances, I cannot
help thinking, whatever arrangement might be made on the
principles of bimetallism, and whatever ratio might be established, gold, and gold alone, will always be chosen as the
favorite, if not the only possible, medium of settling a large
debt, or of making a large remittance for some cause or
other.

" We, *i. e.*, our firm, have on several occasions been
obliged to send a million sterling in sovereigns or bar gold
abroad, which million, when packed up, amounts to a weight
of about ten tons. Is it likely, and, even if desirable, would
it be feasible and practical, supposing a ratio of twenty to
one were established, to send two hundred tons of metal at
one and the same time? It seems to me that the operation
would be impossible, and the sender would therefore naturally
elect, or rather be *compelled*, to send gold, even if it had to be
bought *at a premium.*"

Well, we have then the premium. But the
premium is the death-knell of the system. It

is a death struggle. The Bank of England, the Bank of France, the Bank of Germany, the banks of the United States, all forced into a struggle to keep the gold which is the necessary instrument of their operations, and now very much harder to obtain on account of its increased relative scarcity in comparison with the enormous mass of recently made silver money.

The premium on gold is the death-knell and downfall of universal bimetallism. The struggle for self-protection has begun—the treaties are suspended, free coinage stopped, and the double standard denounced, and liquidation entered upon.

What a liquidation! Following on the eve of enormous silver coinage, and consequently of inflation and speculation such as the world has never seen! Millions and thousands of millions of depreciated coin to be redeemed! and if to be redeemed in gold—universal bankruptcy—universal ruin.

INTERNATIONAL AGREEMENT IMPOSSIBLE.

Is international bimetallism even *possible?* It involves an international agreement between the leading nations. Let us take up the question of the possibility of forming an international agreement. There can be no better indication of this than the attitude of the various governments at the most recent meeting on the subject, the Brussels Conference. At that time, a mild form of advocacy of bimetallism was involved in the following resolution embodied in the program by the United States Government :

" That in the opinion of this Conference it is desirable that some measure should be found for increasing the use of silver in the currency system of the nations."

In speaking upon this resolution and in the further deliberations, there developed the greatest reserve on the part of all but one or two of the delegates present.

The Netherlands supported it without reserve, and advocated pure bimetallism.

So did Mexico.

England placed herself on record as follows :

" Our faith is that of the school of monometallism, pure and simple. We do not admit that any other than the single gold standard would be applicable to our country."

And in substance, further : " Our Government desires to have it known that we do not care to take up the discussion of bimetallism. We decline to accept any invitation to a conference which implies that our Government had any doubt as to the maintenance of the monetary system which has been in force since 1816."

Germany—single gold standard—put herself on record thus:

"Germany being satisfied with its monetary system, *has no intention of modifying its basis.* . . . In view of the satisfactory monetary situation of the Empire, the Imperial Government has prescribed the most strict reserve for its delegates, who, in consequence, cannot take part either in the discussion or in the vote upon the resolution presented by the delegates of the United States."

Austria-Hungary—gold standard:

"Gentlemen, the Conference is not unaware that recently by a series of legislative measures the two States which compose the Austro-Hungarian Empire, have changed their monetary system to the gold standard. In fact, the two countries are at present in a transition period, which explains sufficiently, I hope, the reserve which is forced upon them."

The delegate from Roumania expressed himself as follows:

" Gentlemen, Roumania is one of the group of States which have adopted the gold standard, and the first result of that reform, which was not effected without sacrifices on our part, was to make the agio which in some years had reached twenty-two per cent. disappear immediately." He adds: " How could it be admitted that countries like Germany, England, Austro-Hungary, without speaking of Russia, whose gold reserve increases daily, and which advances with rapid strides toward monometallism should renounce the monetary system and laws which these great powers had adopted only after mature reflection, and after being thoroughly convinced of the advantages to be derived from them."

Holland : " Holland will not enter into a bimetallic union without the full and complete participation of England as a part of the formal instructions furnished us by our Government."

France defined her position as follows, through her delegate : "Why should France permit the coinage of silver when she is already amply provided with it? I believe that she alone possesses as much as all the other States of Europe put together."

"The aspect of the question would be changed if England, the German Empire, Austro-Hungary, the Scandinavian States and others would consent to open their mints to the free coinage of silver (well knowing that this would not be done)."

Latin Union States : The States in the Latin Union held all of them the same views as those expressed by France and Holland.

Sweden : Mr. Hans Forssell of Sweden said,

" Sweden joins with Germany, Austro-Hungary, Great Britain, Switzerland and Russia in refusing to enter into a bimetallic agreement. If the conference of Brussels contributes to establish and fortify the conviction, which is already very general, *that an international agreement for the free and unlimited coinage of silver as full legal tender money is not only rejected for the moment, but inadmissible for the future,* it will have reached a very important result. It will have destroyed the vain and sterile illusions which have already too long troubled men's minds and turned them from the reality of facts, towards the dream of an unrealizable Utopia."

Switzerland : Mr. Cramar Frey, of Switzerland, said,

"As at the conferences of 1878 and 1881, Switzerland continues to consider it as a fixed principle of her monetary policy that there should not be two standards or two measures of value. The most formal instructions from the Swiss Government were to the effect that the Government would not entertain the idea that bimetallism would be admissible for Switzerland."

Italy : Italy voiced her opinion as follows: " It is evident that a higher and almost inevitable law impels civilized nations to pass gradually to gold monometallism. In proportion to their economic progress the intrinsic value of the monetary unit which they adopt must be raised."

I wish I had time to read to you parts of some of the other speeches at this Conference. They are full of expressions of the most determined opposition to bimetallism. The statesmen of Europe will not consent to it and the bimetallists over there have about made up their minds that it is out of the question.

After the Conference had been in session nearly three weeks, Mr. Alphonse Allard, delegate of Belgium and Turkey, one of the most pronounced and intelligent bimetallists present, made the following admission in writing, prefacing a compromise proposal.

He said :

" The obstacles to bimetallism, which it would be useless to pretend not to see, are :

" 1. The enormous difference of thirty-six per cent, between the value of the two metals.

" 2. The gold standard, to which, rightly or wrongly, several important European countries cling.

" 3. The artificial inequality produced by the exchanges, which since they are unfavorable to some, are for that very reason advantageous to others.

" 4. The difficulty of proposing additions to the coinage of those countries which already hold very large stocks of their own silver coins."

Then he adds—and I especially call your attention to this as the conclusion of the whole Conference summed up on the bimetallist side by an enthusiastic advocate of that school :

" If we are to find a remedy for the fall in prices and to increase the stock of money in international circulation, we must coin no more silver ; we must put more silver in circulation : we must keep in view nothing but the *gold standard.*"

This was just about one week before the Conference adjourned, and the intelligent, deliberate, conclusion of a leading bimetallist, after careful consideration of the expressed position of twenty leading nations of the world, gathered together for the special purpose of considering this very subject.

It is conclusive against the practicability of international bimetallism.

9

The nations of Europe are already saturated with silver. They are thoroughly convinced of its inadaptability to the purposes of international commerce, and to repeat Roumania's observation, " How can it be expected that countries like Germany, England, Austro-Hungary and others will renounce the monetary system and laws which these great powers had adopted only after mature reflection and after being thoroughly convinced of the advantages to be derived from them ? "

Gentlemen, they will not do it, and international bimetallism, even if desirable, which it is not, is in this view absolutely impossible.

THE GOLD SUPPLY.

The Bimetallists themselves concede the superiority of the single gold standard if only there is gold enough. On that point all the most recent statistics show a decided increase in gold production all over the world. Stimulated by the needs and conditions as regards gold *vs.* silver, the genius of the century is being turned towards cheapening processes which have already made it profitable to work ore containing only $2.00 in gold per ton. The gold hunter is abroad in all parts of the world.

Murat Halstead says: " The call for the

yellow metal will be answered, the demand
supplied, and we may anticipate the discoveries
of abundance, as in South Africa." Mr. Tran-
ckel, in an elaborate article on the South Africa
field, says :

" It is not impossible that in a few years a
quantity of gold not far from 100,000,000 will
be available for monetary use. If this should
prove true, it would seem futile to speak of an
impending scarcity of gold."

The most recent report is from Professor
Lexis, who has prepared for the Imperial Currency Commission exhaustive statistics of the
gold production of the world. He proves that
the markets of the world may be assured an
average annual supply of 145 millions of dollars
in gold for the next thirty years, and that the
gold currency countries need not fear a scarcity
of the metal.

Well, let us recapitulate. We have seen——

1st. That bimetallism in France was a
failure.

2d. That the fall of prices since 1873 was
not caused by the appreciation of gold.

3d. That it did not bring misery and ruin
in its wake, but, on the contrary, that the
workman in the United States was twice as
well off in 1892 as in 1873, and that since 1873
we have had an era of marvellous prosperity.

4th. That universal bimetallism, even if it could be tried, which it cannot, would bring inflation, the worst scramble for gold ever known, liquidation, and wide-spread ruin.

5th. That the positive refusal of governments at the Brussels Conference to consider bimetallism, proves the absolute impossibility of getting the leading or any other nations together into an international agreement for bimetallism.

6th. That the supply of gold is on the increase, is sufficient, and will continue to be.

UNITED STATES AND THE GOLD STANDARD.

We have one thing more to consider; that is, the position of the United States with respect to the gold standard.

We are the great creditor nation of the world, and can demand what we please in payment. It cannot but be admitted that to-day there is nothing better than gold. Shall we accept an inferior metal, even though we are assured that silver would be *just as good* under International Bimetallism (an untried theory that exploded under partial pressure in 1873)?

The business men of the United States would make short work of it if the question and the facts were brought before *them* for decision.

They would say, as I believe you, gentlemen, are saying to yourselves:

Gold is the best.

We of America are satisfied with gold.

We do not admit for a moment that any other than the Single Gold Standard will do for the United States.

BANKERS AND LEGISLATION.*

THERE was a time, not many years ago, when the banker was content to keep still, and under the ban of curses and objurgations to pursue his quiet course. He would earnestly advise submission, to anyone of the fraternity, who, smarting under injustice, essayed to defend against wrongful accusation or to institute needed reforms. This very submission was in itself an acknowledgment of guilt, and the silence of the banker on the important questions of the day, for the solution of which the public looked to him, has been one of the most potent reasons for the present unsatisfactory condition of our national finances and the existence of our currency troubles.

If, in 1875-6-7 and 8, the bankers and the sound money men had been organized as they are organized now, and had spoken out as they are speaking out now; had started out on a campaign of education as they are starting out now, the Greenback would long ago have been wiped out; the Silver lunacy, before it had

* Before the Banker's Club, Chicago, April 27, 1895.

134

wrought incalculable damage, would have been confined to the asylums where it belongs, and Populism would have been promptly swept back into the holes of its native prairie from which it originally emerged and would have become a rare specimen of this dangerous manifestation of barbarism, which now mouths poisonously against our possessions and our liberties.

LEGISLATION AND BUSINESS.

What ought bankers to do about legislation?

This, it seems to me, is the most important thing for us to-night, or for any body of bankers in this country, to consider and to consider at once. It supersedes all questions of individual management and money making, because the course of legislation at this time is either to make towards a solid foundation on which all future business may be based with success, or failing this, we are to go on upon the vibrating scaffolding which has been our only dependence for many years.

When we come to consider it, what a lamentable condition of affairs we have in the business world of the United States. We have a country teeming with millions of industrious, law-abiding people; we have unlimited resources of earth and air—a rich soil, a favorable climate, immense deposits of mineral wealth, fabulous resources in gas, oil, coal, iron, silver, and gold. With all these advantages we have had to endure the destruction of millions upon millions of property by the blighting fires of panic.

I do not believe that any but the most superficial investigator or a prejudiced demagogue will deny that the trouble at the base is a trouble of currency. Certainly no honest and intelligent student of the facts can arrive at any other conclusion.

THE CURRENCY.

What is wrong with the currency?

In a few words the redemption of our entire volume of paper money falls upon the Treasury —a thousand millions of dollars depending for redemption in gold upon an institution which has no means of getting gold in a legitimate business way to redeem with, has none of the machinery necessary for carrying on the note-issuing business, no automatic way of getting information as to how much money is needed in trade, no possible way of getting that money out when needed, and no way of getting it back if by clumsy chance some gets out.

Like the man with too many notes out, as long as things are prosperous and the revenue is heavy the notes float, but the moment there is a turn and a prospect of insufficient revenue every one wants his notes cashed. The revenue condition then is merely an incident, not the cause of trouble.

We must depend upon legislation to get us out of this condition, because the mistakes of our law-makers through many years have brought us where we are. You are well acquainted with the history of these mistakes. I need only touch upon them.

If there was any experiment in finances, no matter how many times it had exploded in history, the United States was ready to take it up. Some French writer, referring to this, has said that God is good to little children, drunken men, and the people of the United States, and that any other country in the world, under like experiments, would have gone to eternal destruction long ago.

Unlike other great nations, when the peril of war confronted the United States, it had no great financial institution to look to, and its only dependence in a banking way was upon the thousands of small institutions of the country. It turned then in its extremity to the fatal expedient of issuing its own notes, and the seductive poison has never been eradicated. Through misery and destruction we

slowly emerged from the Greenback era after
the heresy had swept more wildly over the
Western plains than the silver heresy is sweep-
ing to-day, after it had taken possession of legislation more wholly than has that to-day. The
glory of resumption of specie payments was
dimmed by the malarial fogs of Bland silver
legislation in 1878, and by the stoppage of cancellation of the Greenback, and the spirit of
compromise with wrong, completed its second
fatal treaty in the Sherman Law of 1890.

Every person in the United States to-day
is suffering more or less from this cancerous
blight of fiat money.

THE SILVER HERESY.

At this juncture, when the struggle of the
Government to maintain its vast obligations in
gold, nearly failing, has through the sagacity
and magnificent courage of President Cleveland been turned over to the strongest bankers
in the world, who are demonstrating daily that
the Government should retire from banking—
at this time, we are confronted once more in organized masses by the silver heresy. I cannot
but feel that this is the last desperate onslought
and that these wild delusionists are making
their last fierce fight before it is too late, feeling that the great American people, quick

scholars as they have always proven, have become educated by the stirring events of the past three years to see things as they are.

On this silver question the American people are beginning to discard the old delusion that law can regulate the value of coin or of anything else; that law, covered with some vague power, can decree that twice one are one, whether it be standard metals, base-balls, or grains of wheat.

WHAT IS THE STANDARD?

They have asked themselves what *must* be the Standard of value, and they have wrought out this answer.

It must be the thing that the largest number of most intelligent people in the community interested, decide that they would rather have for such part of their possessions, as they do not wish, temporarily to put into the form of food, clothes, real estate, and like ownings.

It is, in other words:

What everybody would rather have than anything else.

Put the question to a thousand average people:

"What material thing would you rather have than anything else?"

Answer, "Money."

Question. "What kind of money, Silver or Gold?"

Answer. "Gold."

"Why Gold? Why not Silver?"

"Because Silver is in dispute. Silver is in doubt. There is no doubt about Gold—Gold is the best."

Do you think you can change that opinion by *law?*

Suppose a thousand intelligent educated people in the United States decide that Gold is the best and that they want their money in Gold. Are you going to change that opinion by law? Will an Act of Congress do it? Will the combined command of all the Nations of the Earth do it? And yet that is what the International Bimetallists propose to do. To change intelligent public opinion, the positive conclusion of a vast army of people skilled in Commerce, to change by act of law, a verdict which has been arrived at through the operations and development of Commerce through the· ages—a development which in the last thirty years has been amazingly rapid. To change all that, and waving back the great brainy crowd that do the business of the world, do it with marvellous skill, intelligence and honor, say to them : "You do not know what you are talking about ; silver is as good as gold. We declare it to be so, and you must accept this declaration as final."

These men, it seems to me, are assuming the functions of the Almighty.

DELUSION OF INTERNATIONAL BIMETALLISM.

Then comes the theorist with the honey of philanthropy on his tongue and the distress, wrought by the very thing he advocates, before his eyes, and says: " What are you going to do about falling prices? Don't you want prosperity everywhere? Don't you all want to be happy? "

These are the illusions of Utopia.

You can't help falling prices at times.

You can't have prosperity everywhere all the time.

You can't all be happy always in a material way.

You ask how to avoid the ills of shrinking prices and the hardships of fluctuating exchanges that come in trade.

They cannot be avoided altogether, any more than you can avoid, altogether, sickness and death. Improved methods of living may be adopted, microbes and bacilli for numberless diseases discovered and eradicated by antidote, but sickness and death come at last to the strongest constitutions. It is natural law. Legislation cannot cure it. The same thing is true in trade. There is as much clap-trap about the programme of the International Bi-metallist, as there is in that of the circus doctor selling his universal "cure all." And this International Bimetallist has wrought incalculable harm with his specious theory, his high educational atmosphere, his charming oratory. He has led men who had no time to think to believe that the rose-colored theory must be true, because honesty and intellect endorsed it.

It is time to tear off disguise. International Bimetallism is a traitor in the camp. It is a false fraud. It can never be accomplished. It is a Will-o'-the Wisp dancing above the deadly marsh. It is as elusive as a dream of magic; as idle as the pursuit of perpetual motion; as dangerous as the delirium of Fiat Money.

If it could ever be accomplished, which, thanks to the inability of several great Nations to agree, it never can be, what would be the consequences?

A TRIAL OF UNIVERSAL BIMETALLISM.

The mints of the World would be open at the ratio of sixteen to one to anyone who cared to bring silver bullion, and to any extent. Anyone bringing forty to fifty cents worth of silver

bullion could carry away a dollar. Do you
know of any better business than that—sixty
cents on the dollar clear profit? Production of
silver would be stimulated enormously. It has
been estimated that the annual output would
rise from $200,000,000 to $400,000,000. The
producer with his $600 profit on every $1000,
would carry away his bagsful, and everybody
would have to receive his fiat silver dollar
under the glorious international law. Where
would they go? Out of the pockets and safes
into the Banks, and then? More and more
encumbered and embarrassed by the bulky
silver they would seek to get rid of it, utterly
unfitted as it is for large payments which the
Banks are expected to make. Then would
come the struggle for gold—and then the
Premium.

But Premium means dissolution to Bimetallism, a death struggle between the great Banks
of the world to retain Gold the only instrument
of the liquidation which would follow the downfall of Universal Bimetallism. Liquidation!
after the enormous coinage of silver brought
on by the international experiment and following as it would a period of inflation and speculation such as the world has never known—
liquidation?—redemption in Gold of thousands
upon thousands of millions of depreciated coin?

it would be an attempt at the Impossible; it
would accomplish only one thing—Universal
Bankruptcy and Ruin.

THE BANKERS' PART.

In these times when such things are preached
as good doctrine, when sound money principles
are sapped and weakened by such suggestions
of compromise with the silver lunacy as International Bimetallism, it seems to me that plain
words are best. Gentlemen, I am here to-
night to talk over with you the question of
what should be our part in this fight. Because
the fight is on ; this is War for Education and
all disguise should be thrown off.

The Banker has a large influence if he would
only use it. He is the confidential advisor of
thousands and thousands of business men.
The business men of the United States, a great
class, are peaceable, industrious, intelligent
citizens, and the mainstay of this country as
against fanaticism and demagogism. The
laboring element comes closely in contact
with these business men. The prosperity of
the latter means the prosperity of the daily
wage earner. Now the banker's part is to
make his clients thoroughly understand the
issue at stake and the effect of Heresy upon
trade. To do this, he must himself be well
informed, and every Banker in these times

should go to the bottom of these questions. He should take a firm stand on the highest plane of sound money principles.

It is a time for aggressive action, and the bankers could do a great work if they would organize sound money clubs in every community, including business, professional, and working men. These could perfect and carry out programmes for talks and conferences. Education by pamphlet and speech could be carried on.

A DEFENSIVE UNION

Once created, the clubs could unite under a central head similar to the one just formed in Germany, a "Union for the Defence of the Gold Standard," admitting representatives from all the leading Chambers of Commerce. This action would soon make itself felt in the political tide. The politician would be made to feel that the sentiment of the great intelligent majority is for sound money, and that in heeding the call of the Populist, or even in endeavoring to conciliate the Silverite, he is conspiring for his own downfall. These are the things the banker could accomplish, and no one could more widely disseminate sound doctrine, more earnestly make known the simple requisites of sound money, the essential requirements in currency for solid prosperity, than he. In the counting-room, in consultation with his own customers, at the Board of Trade, and at the banquet, he could make himself heard and felt, and would become a tower of strength for the conservation of what is right in money. A new sentiment would blaze from one end of the land to the other; a sentiment which, once established, would mean quick legislation in the right direction, and a satisfactory settlement of the currency question in the United States for all time. And the sentiment which would thus be crystallized by the organized work of the bankers, and the fact that would be demonstrated and which is true to-day, would be this:

THE POLITICAL PARTY THAT PANDERS TO FREE SILVER, OR THAT WITH A REPUTATION FOR BEING A SOUND PARTY, ENDEAVORS TO TAKE A MIDDLE COURSE ON THE MONEY QUESTION BETWEEN SOUND AND UNSOUND MONEY, IS DOOMED AND DESERVES TO BE.

And this other:

THE POLITICIAN, HIGH OR LOW, WHO TO-DAY TURNS FROM THE STRAIGHT COURSE OF SOUND MONEY AND THE GOLD STANDARD, STABS DEAD ONCE FOR ALL HIS EVERY CHANCE FOR POLITICAL SUCCESS, *especially if he wants to be president.*

THE STATE BANK QUESTION.*

THE commercial interests of the United States demand a circulating medium adequate to the great business of the country.

Instead of this, the currency situation is one of the most complicated and unsatisfactory which our national life has produced.

Thus far in the history of the world, every attempt by a government to create paper currency has brought discomfiture and disaster. It is because of governmental interference in the issue of paper money that we, in the United States, are in our present uncomfortable dilemma.

The politicians, urged on by the complaints of their constituents, are groping after some panacea which is afar off, and because some of the features of the old State bank system embodied a likeness to the true principle of circulation, one great political party has uneasily turned toward that as a refuge for answer to the cry of commerce for better things.

* Appeared originally in Rhodes's *Journal of Banking* for October, 1892.

What is the true principle of circulation? What is the perfect currency?

In answer to this question we go over the old ground.

It must be absolutely secure.

It must be of uniform value throughout the country.

It must be convertible into gold.

And last of all, especially in this country, it should be elastic in volume, expanding or contracting at need.

Does the National Bank system furnish such a currency?

If not, will the revival of State bank circulation do it?

In answer to the first question, I beg to repeat from a former article, that norwithstanding the popular notion that our National bank currency is the best the world ever knew, it is a fact that the unscientific character of that currency is the very thing that has brought us to the present uncomfortable condition of our finances; that is to say, the rate-reduction and redemption of Government bonds (the pledging of any comparatively short-lived security like a Government bond being necessarily disturbing) has caused thus far by retirement of National notes a contraction of over $230,-000,000 in our currency, and just at a time

when more currency has been needed. This
has made it possible for the silver scheme to
gain such preposterous headway in this country, and under the guise of supplying the great
commercial need of *more currency*, has flooded
us with the baser metal.

This brings us to the fault of bonds as a
basal security. The currency of a country
should be based upon actual possessions, not
upon public debt—upon wealth, not upon poverty—and a bond, Government or State, is an
evidence of *public debt*, not of public property.

Further than this, the system, having for
its principle, *special* security, that is, security
pledged and held specially, as are our government bonds, is defective in a country requiring sensitive elasticity in its currency. Such
a system fails to respond to the laws of trade,
and under it the volume of currency, if there
is a profit in it, will be too great, and if there is
no profit it will shrink without regard to the
needs of the community. These two conditions have both at different times confronted us.

Then, too, because the National notes are
specially secured, there never was any actual
daily redemption of them in the natural course
of trade, and this great controlling feature is
lost to the system.

I have said that we need in this country a currency specially sensitive in the quality of elasticity, besides being absolutely secure. On account of great field and forest production, we require at certain seasons of the year a rapid and substantial increase in our medium of exchange, the volume of which should, to avoid inflation, as rapidly shrink when the need is past.

What have we actually got for currency in the United States? With what is left of the National bank notes and our vastly increased and ever-increasing Government issues, we have, as far as elasticity is concerned, a sodden, unyielding mass. There is not one first principle of elasticity in it. Our present system is a vast financial cyclone breeder. Under it when confidence is felt, the excess of money provokes speculation and inflation. But when confidence shrinks there is no natural relief, and we get a panic.

Will the State Bank system do any better things for us? Let us see what would be accomplished by turning on State circulation. Banking before the war was largely experimental. Each State tried one thing or another with variable degrees of success. A few of the States struck the right principle, and in two or three, for a period of forty years, the most exemplary success was achieved and maintained.

To particularize : the State of Louisiana had such wise laws for its banking department that its system was a model of stability and its currency good. Three States, Ohio, Kentucky, and Indiana, under a system of currency based on commercial assets, maintained a secure and successful position for years without loss to the community who handled their banknotes. The system of New England, with its central redemption agent, the Suffolk Bank of Boston, was perhaps the most peculiarly successful and practically safe of all. Notes were issued on general commercial security, and entailed no loss to noteholders for the whole period of existence, which was terminated only by the imposition of the ten per cent. tax. The system of New York was like our National system, based on the false principle of special security, bonds and mortgages being first pledged, and State bonds afterwards substituted. The system, like our National one, was unscientific and a failure, in that it was obliged to suspend (in 1857), although the notes were all redeemed eventually.

In other States there was no marked success, and in the majority the most decided lack of it. There never was any uniformity of system between States, and as to safety, in twenty or more the windiest thing in the State was banking.

If it is expected by reviving these varying systems to make such a national currency as we need, the expectation will only be fulfilled after a long period of evolution. It is just as sensible to expect to plow a field with thirty wild colts harnessed in with a few staid old farm horses. Of course the colts can be trained.

So it seems there is no relief to be expected from that quarter.

Reverting again to the requirements of commerce, the question arises, " What is the natural basis for a scientific currency?" The answer is not a new one, but nevertheless true.

The wealth of a country should be the basis of its currency. The basis is furnished by commerce itself.

The products of the labor of the people represent all there is of financial value (wealth) in a nation. Commercial banks are the custodians of the representatives of this wealth in the shape of commercial assets, and commercial assets, all time proves, are the highest form of security for note circulation.

Now it is because some of the old State systems involved a part of the principle here laid down, and because the old State systems gradually perfected in all the States on the best models in this or that State, would slowly but certainly, after many years of delay and loss, have reached something approaching the perfected system of our friends the Canadians; it is because of this, and because such men as Russell, the Massachusetts member of the Chicago Platform Committee, and Harter, and others recognized this, that the State-bank plank was introduced into the Democratic platform—a good move from one point of view, because of the vigorous discussion of the question which has ensued, and which will ensue— a discussion which cannot but educate the people.

Admitting that the most perfect form of currency is the note of a good bank, how can you get your banks good before you allow them to issue?

Not certainly by throwing the control of them into the hands of forty-four different Legislatures of all degrees of intelligence and political complexion, as would be done if the State tax were repealed.

For twenty-nine years the National system has been perfecting its restrictions until to-day it shows a high standard of average strength and safety, and a record for the whole period of its existence which probably—taking number of banks and all into consideration—is unequalled in the history of banking. This record is condensed in the statement that the total average of loss in the whole system for the whole time is only three per cent.

Here, then, is a system which on one side has been developed and perfected with the utmost care for twenty-nine years by a succession of competent comptrollers, until on that side— the Department of Safety—it has attained a very high level. On the other side, that most important one—of circulation—there has been actually no development whatever. On the contrary, that limb of the system has become a withered member. The paralysis which set in there as soon as Government bonds got out of sight as rate-payers, was allowed to continue without the skilful attendance of those who alone should have been allowed to prescribe— a Committee of expert bankers and financial men. The currency doctors, of which no other nation on earth has as many as we, were allowed to get in their work, controlled and owned, as they were, by the silver men, who saw their opportunity in a lack of circulating medium to foist their metal upon the people, and to-day we oscillate at dizzy height on the feather edge of a change from gold to silver standard, with millions of the baser metal on hand to tip the balance toward disaster.

We must go back now to the period when the circulation of the National system first began to fail and apply remedies that should then have been used.

The State bank system was a spotted growth from bad to better, with the right principle of note-issue as a general basis in some of the States. But to go back twenty-nine years, tear down the delicate net-work of safety which has developed around the national system, and by a repeal of the ten per cent. tax start over again, would be a crude and unwise move—a retrogression—unnecessary, because every good feature of State bank issue can be grafted on to the strong and efficient trunk of the National system.

If commercial assets, held as general security by making bank-notes a first lien upon the assets, are the best basis for note circulation, why should not that system, regulated and perfected, be adopted and developed by the National banks? The double liability of stockholders would be a further security, and a redemption fund could be perpetuated by yearly tax. Add to this *actual daily redemption* at all of the great cities, and the retirement of currency not needed would be ensured and parity maintained.

We would then have a secure, elastic, convertible, and uniform currency. Dangerous

Government issues could be stopped, and commerce growing, would grow its own circulating medium.

The argument then condensed is this:

1. We need a better currency system.

2. The State bank systems were varied, a few only being successful, but those few possessed the right and vital principle of circulation.

3. The National bank system is strong in nearly all vital particulars except circulation.

4. Combine the right principle of circulation, the best part of the State systems, with the National system, and you have the highest safety and the best currency—an almost perfect whole.

To-day enterprise is stifled by uncertainty. Foreign buying is sluggish, lacking confidence. Money in large amounts has been for a long time congested at the centres, idle, and waiting.

To banish uncertainty,

To restore confidence,

To inaugurate an era of continuing prosperity, two things are needed to be done. Let the people thoroughly understand this, and they will insist upon it.

First—REPEAL THE SILVER BILL OF 1890 (and that alone would make it possible for a long time to do nothing else).

Second—GRAFT THE PRINCIPLE OF NOTE ISSUES BY BANKS (a first lien and secured by general assets) UPON THE NATIONAL BANKING SYSTEM.

The party that inaugurates these moves will merit enduring power.

The politicians who urge and accomplish them will win honest and substantial fame.

THE MONEY POWER*

WHEN your Chairman invited me to speak
to you, he said to me that a few months
ago he intended to vote for McKinley, but that
since the free-silver movement had come up, he
had been told that the money power was working for McKinley and he did n't know but that
was a reason for not voting for him, although he
had not decided, and anyway he really wanted
to be enlightened.

Now, I do not hesitate to say that the money
power *is* for McKinley and the Gold Standard.

But I follow this up with the inquiry, " What
is the money power in this country ? " and with
this reply :

" The money power is the power that furnishes and controls the cash and the cash credits
of the United States."

This power is concentrated in the hands of
the Banks, the Loan Associations, the Mort-
gage Companies, and the Insurance Companies.
There are a few individual bankers, but they
are in a small minority.

* Address during the Presidential Campaign, 1896.

158

I have mentioned first the Banks.

What is a Bank?

A Bank is one of the machines of business.

The capital is generally furnished by hundreds of people, most of them in moderate circumstances, who take shares of stock and put in the money to start with.

The greater part of the Bank's money is, however, the property of small depositors and business men, hundreds and thousands of them for each Bank, and the average amount placed on deposit by each is small. Taken all together, however, the whole makes up a very large sum which the Bank Officer is expected to loan out and invest safely, but must always be ready to pay back to the depositor in cash.

Remember, then, the Banker, against whom we hear so much abuse from ignorant quarters, is the paid servant who looks after the interests of the entire institution, the interests of thousands of people in each institution. And, although he must have more experience than the man who digs, or the man who takes care of horses, he is, nevertheless, " a hired man."

When Mr. Bryan was in Buffalo, he took special pains to stigmatize Bankers, but in his speech in New York, and in all his speeches, he has shown such great ignorance on the subject of banking, that I am inclined to think that it is his age more than anything else that is at fault. I remember when I was about as old as he is (and I had then been in the Banking business more than half my life), I knew a great many things about Banking which I have since learned were not so.

Now youth is a magnificent quality, but it is better on a Ranch than in an Executive Chair, especially if such things have to be said, as have to be, concerning Mr. Bryan, namely, for instance, that what he knows about Finance *is not so*, and that in all his ninety-seven speeches in the "enemies' country," speeches teeming with crowns, crosses, firebrands and revolution, appealing, as they do, to the dangerous element, not one of his arguments will stand the test of calm, cool investigation, based on facts and experience.

And, now, what does the Banker do with the money left in his care.

He loans it out judiciously to the business man and manufacturer in the place where the Bank is located, and it helps these to do business, to increase their plants, to employ labor and so to get money into circulation.

And this, my friends, is the only way to get money into circulation in the United States. The farmer will tell you that he wants to see "more money in circulation." Well it can't be

done without the business man is prosperous
and employs labor that spends and eats, and
without the business man is prosperous, the
Banks cannot be prosperous.

The Bankers, then, of the United States, are,
mainly, trustees of the people's money, employed on salary, and expected to so conduct
the affairs of the Banks that the greatest benfit
will come to their stockholders, to their depositors, to the whole business of the locality,
by means of careful loaning.

Remember, now, each Bank, Savings Bank
and Trust Company is made up in about the
same way.

Let us take them all together and add the
Building and Loan Associations, which come
under the same class.

We have in round figures:

	Amount.	No. of people.	Av. each.
Savings Banks Deposits,	$1,810,597,000	4,875,000	$371.00
State Banks, Trust Companies and Private Banks,	1,340,888,000	1,500,000	900.00
National Banks, with whom 1,724,000 persons have less than $1,000 each to his credit,	1,701,653,000	1,929,000	
Building and Loan Associations,	500,000,000	1,800,000	280.00

or, all in together, five thousand three hundred and fifty millions of dollars, owned by ten millions of thrifty people—owning, many of them, only a few dollars apiece, and, at the average, only about $500 apiece.

This is the money power.

Listen. It is early morning in the great City. Do you hear that sound of footsteps on the cool stones—shuff—shuff, hundreds, thousands, stepping, stepping, regularly, increasingly, through the marts and highways where commerce flows ?

These are they who carry the dinner-pail ; the laborers, the shop-girls, the clerks, the vast army of the employed ; millions and millions of them.

This is the money power.

They do not drive on the boulevards. They do not live lives of ease and luxury. They do service wherever commerce needs a willing hand, a clear head, a thrifty soul.

The man next to you, you yourself, the man with the pick-axe, the bookkeeper behind that long desk, the girls in the store, the factory hands, the man who owns the corner grocery, that old woman there knitting behind the pile of vegetables which she has for sale and which she has raised with her own hands ; the tin-smith who is pounding the music of industry out of that great winding strip of tin at his bench ; the widow woman whose little fund in the savings bank, added to the work of her hands, keeps her above want.

This is the money power. All there is of thrift, industry, virtue, the good old-fashioned qualities that make a nation great—these are the reasons of the existence of this great army —" the potentates of the dinner-pail."

They own the hundreds of millions in our Savings Banks, they hold the foremost lien upon the assets of our great Life Insurance Companies. They are the shareholders in the Loan Associations, and, in the aggregate, each owning a little, are heavy stockholders in our great railway corporations and industrials.

The country's wealth is distributed among them, they are relatively rich, and there never was a time in any age or in any land when these wage earners received so much for their toil and could buy so much with what they received as they could from 1879 to 1890, when the gold basis in the United States was a sure thing and everybody thought so.

They are the money power. They, the industrious, thrifty, money-saving people of this country. They furnish the cash and cash credits which make the power, and that is why the money power is for gold—for an honest dollar—against repudiation—against revolution.

It is a question of self-preservation.

An attack has been made upon their property.

An attempt is being made to get them to consent to cut in two the savings of years.

To take these dollars, for each of which they have given one hundred cents in the sweat of the brow and legislate half of it away.

My friends do you think they will consent to this?

The honesty and thrift of the Green Mountains has already answered the question.

Their answer is 39,000 thundering *Noes*.

ABRAHAM LINCOLN*

WORDS have small power to bear out the thoughts and memories which crowd around us to-day in the shadow of this sacred tomb.

And foremost as we stand here there comes that vision of the funeral pageant, the solemn procession that wound its way for sixteen hundred miles, while a nation looked upon its beloved, cold and dead, and, to view the venerated one on the way to the tomb, flocked by day and night, in the cool dawn, at full noon, when the solemn twilight was settling, and by the ruddy glare of torches in the night, and at his bier the people mourned uncomforted, and the whole Nation throbbed like one heart with aching sorrow.

The mystery of life and death is made doubly wonderful here by the life and character of this mighty one.

Gentle, merciful, full of humor, friend of the

* Address at Springfield, Ill., before the American Bankers' Association at the tomb of Lincoln, Sept., 25, 1896.

homely and the unfortunate, courageous, just, forgiving, fertile in resources, unerringly wise. Seeing final effects far ahead, with wonderful knowledge of men, the power of his intellect moulded irresistibly the circumstances that presented themselves, and let them come stronger, so he grew stronger to meet them and to mould them his way.

He is called the greatest intellectual force of our time, one of the world's greatest men, and withal tender in heart and full of yearning pity for the downcast, even the dumb animals. This quality of tenderness, and sympathy with the simple, so impressed itself upon the people who knew him and the humble ones with whom he came in contact, that there grew around his memory a halo of romance. Why, the farmer's of central Illinois around here will tell you to this day that the brown thrush did not sing for a year after he died.

But this tolerant justice extended to those in good circumstances, to the prosperous and wealthy, as well as to the poor. This appeals especially to us at this time when abuse of the Fortunate and the Thrifty is so common. Full of enthusiasm to accomplish, to right wrongs, he yet worked with utmost caution, diplomacy, statesmanship. His patience, as his biographers truly say, was like that of Nature—a vast and fruitful activity but knowing neither haste nor rest.

In days like these in which we live, when the very life of our Republic is threatened by wild theories, revolutionary platforms and appeals to hate, sedition and dishonor, we turn to our great ideals for comfort, to the heroes and the heroic epochs of our native history for encouragement and for inspiration—and we do not turn in vain.

If we look to our greatest name and the record of the time of Lincoln, before he had taken up the leadership, we find that a greater emergency confronted us in those days. Rebellion had become rampant in those four months between November of the election and March of the inauguration. Difficult as were his future tasks (through four long years when opposition, calumny, misrepresentation, bore down upon him) none were more so or required more consummate skill and wisdom than the Deliverance of those early days of '61 ; the crystallization of the Union from out the chaos of secession in which it was apparently inextricably involved.

God raised up this Leader then, not in a day but through years of trying discipline, to lead the people ; through a heritage of hardship and sorrow—out of privation and ignorance—came this great intellect—a light to lead a people out of darkness and bondage, a Nation out of the throes of dissolution, into strong Unity. A Nation that can produce such a man and that has come through such an ordeal under his guidance ; that fully appreciates the character of that struggle and the character of the hero that led them, can never decide wrong on any such question as that which to-day confronts it.

Seeds of sedition and revolution are hourly cast broadcast from the throats of those who, let us in charity say, know not what they do.

Appeals for degradation and National dishonor fly on the voice and on the wire from State to State.

In this situation the mind cannot but revert to another time when a demagogue, on Union soil, in a series of public addresses, surpassed all bounds in traitorous denunciation of the government and in malicious vituperation of the Union.

Then, as now, crowds flocked to hear him ; but when the time for ballots came Vallandigham was swept out of sight by the largest majority old Ohio ever gave.

That great people, who through four years of battle days—through ordeal of blood and fire,— worked out that wonderful salvation, Freedom for the Slave and Unity and Honor for the State, will never give up the heritage so dearly bought, will never allow the National banners to be stained with repudiation and tarnished credit.

History will repeat itself, and the disturbers of public law and order, the breeders of mass and class revolution, the pleaders for dishonesty and National dishonor, will be swept to oblivion by the greatest majority this country has ever known.

His great spirit looks down upon us to-day. Here rests the Moses of the people who after the four years of terrible trial, when victory was won, and the bells were ringing out the sweet hymns of peace, was allowed, only to look upon the promised land—not to enter in. But a higher glory and reward were reserved for him.

He has entered into the eternal rest and his great spirit looks down complacently upon our struggle, with sure knowledge of the outcome.

My friends let us humbly imitate him in the honest work we are doing for the Nation's honor. In his own words, almost his last, "With malice towards none, with charity for all, with firmness in the right as God gives us to see the right, let us strive on to finish the work we are in."

THE END

INDEX.

Act of 1873, 28
Action, necessity for, 82, 145
Africa, South, 105
Allard, M. Alphonse, 128
American Bankers' Association, 51, 165
Americans quick scholars, 138
Appeal to Congress, 38
Assignat, 93
Atkinson, Edward, 103, 106, 115, 116
Austria, at Brussels conference, 126
Austrian Special Commission, 93
A way out, 79, 86
A wild chase, 48

Baltimore plan, 82, 84, 86, 87, 88
Bank currency, progress, 62 ; large banks only to issue, 18
Bank, machinery development, 71 ; machinery economizes all
  business, 71, what is a, 68, 159 ; notes, 15, 82
Bank note suppression, 59, 66
Bank notes, first lien, 15, 62 ; and checks identical, 71 ; how
  they operate, 76 ; increase and decrease, 16 ; national, good
  enough, 84 ; security, 17
Bank of England, 123
Bank officer, 159
Banker paid servant, 69, 159
Bankers and legislation, 134
Bankers' Club, Chicago, 134
Bankers part, 144 ; trustees, 161 ; silence, 134
Banking, and currency house comm., 73, 82 ; by government
  should cease, 68, 69
Banking business, 69 ; why government unfit for, 11, 70, 73
Bankruptcy universal, 124, 144
Banks, dependence of small, 137 ; injury to, is injury to com-
  munity, 69 ; to get good, 60
Barometer, the reserve is, 34

ments in, 138 ; reform, 51 ; issued by government an abuse,
52 ; issued by government, causes cry more money, 11, 77 ;
issued by government, a failure, 1, 10, 53, 136 ; remedies,
61, 67, 77 ; represents products, 53, 152 ; tool of trade, 70,
71 ; true principle, 148 ; trade unhindered when currency
is sound, 65 ; volume, 64 ; war, 8

www.ingramcontent.com/pod-product-compliance
Lightning Source LLC
Chambersburg PA
CBHW020537270326
41927CB00006B/613